Across the Sound of Sleat

by

Margaret Grant

ISBN 978-1-904-499-41-1

Further copies of this book may be obtained from:
Kirsteen Grant
kirsteen7@btinternet.com

First published in United Kingdom of Great Britain in 2015 by
Roundtuit Ltd t/a Roundtuit Publishing, Portland House , Belmont Business Park, Belmont, Durham DH1 1TW. Company registered in England and Wales. Company number 9519412

Printed in the UK by Glasgow Print + Design Centre
www.GlasgowPDC.co.uk

Contents

I am back

List of Photos

Front cover – Looking to Knoydart from Sleat

Map of the Sound of Sleat

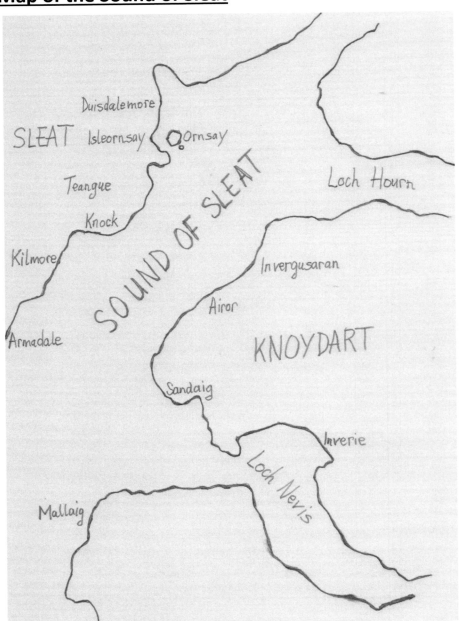

Margaret at home at Ailsa, Camuscross

PREFACE

My mother, Margaret Grant (nee MacInnes), was born in 1912 in Cardross, Dunbartonshire, the daughter of Margaret MacKinnon of Camuscross, Sleat, Skye, and Donald MacInnes of Airor, Knoydart, whose family had gone there from Sleat a couple of generations before. In no 40 Camuscross, my cousin and his family is now the eighth generation of Mother's family to stay there, and from there one can see across the Sound of Sleat the houses in the small village of Airor. Donald, like so many, left Airor for employment, and he and Margaret spent many happy years in Cardross, he as butler at Kilmahew Castle to the Allan family of the well-known shipping line. Both sides

2

benefitted from the appointment – the Allans were fair and generous employers, and I believe my Grandfather was a hard-working, reliable and faithful employee. My Mother's childhood, with an older brother and sister and two younger sisters, was a very happy one at Kilmahew Cottage, her parents being strict, yet kind.

Yet the background in both Knoydart and Skye was always very prominent in their lives, and Mum remembered the many times a dumpling was made to go round a tableful of unexpected visitors who would arrive from either of the northern homelands. Holidays were always "two-centre", with the excitement of the train journey from Cardross to Mallaig. Mum recalled the uncoupling at Crianlairich of the two sections of the train for Oban and Mallaig, and the three young sisters in tears because "Papa" had gone to purchase tea from the café on the platform. They thought they would never see him again! From Mallaig, there was usually an Airor visit first, commencing with a welcoming, scratchy kiss from one of their bearded uncles. Going across to Skye was rather more interesting for the youngsters, as there was plenty of young company in the summers at Camuscross.

Mum married Donald Grant, also from Camuscross, and they made their home in Milngavie and Glasgow, with my brother, Innes, born first and myself to follow. Like our Mother, we also had happy holidays in Skye, although not as extended. By then the house in Airor was empty, and later in the 80's, I remember Mum's indignation on a trip across from Camuscross, where she spent twenty years after Dad's retirement from teaching in Glasgow, at finding goats within the building. Happily, the house has been restored and is being lived in again by a young family. It was only a few years ago that I made my first, exciting trip to Airor.

Mum was a lively, energetic and kindly character, of independent mind, yet always putting others first. Sadly the excitement and happiness of buying no 1 Camuscross on Dad's retirement from teaching in Glasgow was changed dramatically by his sudden death a year later, but she remained in Skye for twenty years, and made a large contribution to the community.

Ailsa, 1 Camuscross, Mum and Dad's retirement home

Although a pensioner, her "taxi service" was known well by her many friends, as well as impromptu picnics and runs all over the island. In my married home in Glasgow, I had to be very prepared for the arrival of the green Morris Minor, which managed 143,000 miles with Mum at the wheel. When Kilmore Church of Scotland was threatened with being merged with Broadford, it was Margaret who led the fund-raising and protest, which successfully kept the church open and independent.

Although she was very proud of her training in Daly's of Sauchiehall Street in Glasgow, I always thought that she would have enjoyed the opportunity to have further education. She was a talented writer, stemming from her keen observation of people and her huge interest in so many areas of life. She was also a leader of people, from the Sales of Work of the Glasgow Skye Association, or whichever other of the many Highland groups in which she and Dad were involved, to the organising of Red Cross outings which, at the age of ninety, she cajoled, persuaded or bullied her fellow residents at the Abbeyfield Residential Home to participate in.

She spent many, many hours working on the "sloinneadh" or family history, before this pastime ever became fashionable, and before the internet made such information so much more accessible. I think she might have laughed at how easily one can come by facts that she had to spend hours researching – or, more likely, she would have grasped the new opportunities with alacrity, had they come twenty years earlier.

Along with a forestation of family trees, five branches going back to the 1700's, she left, it seemed to me, an even more interesting account of her memories and her findings of the social side of her history, and, with her lively mind, not afraid to speak what she thought, she includes her own illuminating observations. The names on the trees begin to take on personalities and become ancestors that you can associate with.

Life was not always straight-forward with a strong mother and perhaps an equally determined daughter, but I gather these writings with immense pride and fondness for the memory of the rich character who was my Mother.

Acknowledgements I have been telling myself to complete this project since Mum died in 2006, and various people have borne the brunt of my efforts.

Thanks to Marrion, my sister-in-law, who has provided some of her own beautiful photos of Skye. Also to my brother, Innes, who has been very patient when receiving regular phone calls to his home on Skye, asking him to look for photos and other information.

To my late Aunt Neilina for painting such a lovely picture of their childhood home at Kilmahew. Painting was a hobby she took up in later life with some success.

To the Sleat Local History Society for photos from their excellent website.

To Carolyn, my good cousin in the USA, for the warm piece about her Grandmother and Grandfather's settling on the other side of the Atlantic.

To my very good friend, Seonaid, who has spent many hours using her expertise, cropping photos, moving photos, "wrapping" script, and sundry other manoeuvres, well beyond my technically-starved brain.

To Iain, my patient husband, who has provided all the basic knowledge and help in scanning and searching, also providing special photos, and has kept the house running when no-one else was doing so.

To Philip Wilson of the Glasgow Print & Design Centre for his informed advice.

But especially to Mum for taking the time, and having the imagination to preserve an account of an era all too easily lost.

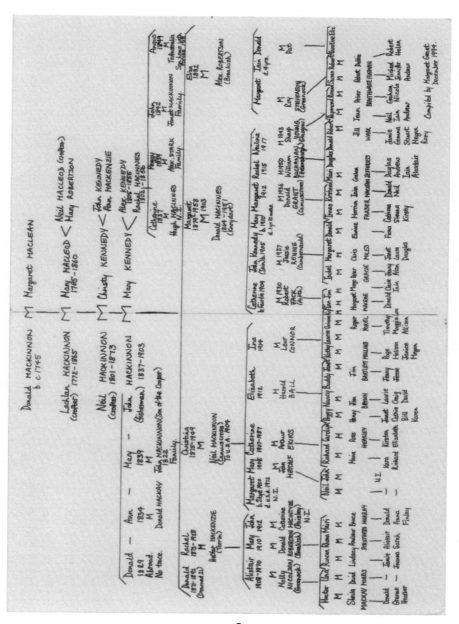

Tree 2

C1745

Johnatton MacInnes
|
Angus MacInnes
1817?91 Boundalamore
m
Margaret Matthew
B1796/Skean
} To River Furydack 1835.

John 1835

1. Cardross

Margaret Ann Grant, born 8/11/1912 at Kilmahew Cottage, Cardross to Maggie MacKinnon and Donald MacInnes. A happy home, with a caring mother and father. Strict in many ways – but fair.

Kilmahew Cottage, painted by Neilina – a hobby she took up in her later years

Most of our living was spent in our kitchen, a fairly spacious room with a door into the front hall and front door – a window looking over to Langbank and another on to the Firth of Clyde, Roseneath Castle and almost Dunoon. The fireplace a range, black-leaded, steel-fronted, a mantelpiece above with a suspended brass rail (handy for airing). In front a beautiful steel fender, full length, with a large poker and tongs resting on either side. My father made a wooden cover for this, and I have a cameo of a Sunday evening with Rachel and Neilina (sisters) sitting on either end of the fender cover on cushions and all of us singing hymns from a red-covered hymn book – Moody and Sankey – including "Dare to be a Daniel" etc. None of us could sing – it must have been an awful sound!

Standing : Neilina, Margaret, Iain, Rachel
Seated : Margaret (mother), Donald (father), Cathie

Every second Sunday Katie Anderson would join with us, her half-day off from Campbell Martin, Drumhead, where she was table-maid. She was distantly related to Mother and her sister married my father's cousin, Jimmy MacKinnon. During Katie's time at Drumhead I grew to be working in Glasgow, and I and my friends paid many pleasant visits to Drumhead.

Another cameo. Moonlight night, Mother and three girls to Drumhead, crossing two fields, along the hedge-line. Father off his work earlier met us

9

on the road on our return. That is the way we were as a family. We were strictly brought up.

Mother had been brought up in the Free Church, of which her mother was a known and respected stalwart. Father was Church of Scotland, of which he became an adherent, but never a member, as was the custom at that time. We followed the old tradition (as much as possible), brushed our shoes for Sunday on a Saturday night, prepared soup and mutton – but I'm sure we boiled the potatoes, left ready on the Saturday, on Sunday.

Margaret and Donald at the door of Kilmahew

Mother was an excellent cook, baker, housewife and dress-maker. For years she made our dresses, skirts and jumpers. Another cameo. Rachel and Neilina at Jimmy MacKinnon's wedding in wine-coloured coats with imitation-fur collars and pinky peach dresses with rucking round the neck Rachel was roughly thirteen, Neilina eleven.

I was working in Daly's by that time and staying during the week in Glasgow with Maggie MacKay, Mother's cousin. A kind benevolent lady, who had a two-room and kitchen house in Maryhill. She and her daughter, Nan, who was in charge of a beautiful jewellers in Glasgow Arcade, slept in the kitchen concealed bed, James, her mother's brother, a bachelor, slept in the bedroom which was his room and I slept in the parlour bed, also concealed with a curtain. Sometimes I had Aunt Teenie as companion between light jobs to oblige old employers.

I was lucky. Maggie was a kind woman, an excellent cook and had a sense of humour, although she was deaf and used a trumpet. She liked me to sing "Danny Boy" into it! Told you she was kind! Mind you, I fitted in quite well. I was quite good at washing the beautifully-tiled close (wally close), washing windows and darning. Happy days travelling back and forward on the train, even for lunch. Later I made use of my bed there when going out with Donald, giving me extra time in Glasgow. Had to waken Maggie that first Christmas when I got my watch from Donald and debate whether I should keep it or not. There was, to me, something final about it.

Schooldays I thoroughly enjoyed. Our infant teacher, Miss MacKinlay, so initiated me to school that I had no traumas about it. The years of "perfect attendance" spoke well to that, though we had a mile and a quarter to get there. We carried "pieces" and the result was we were starving by the time we got home, a lovely cooking smell greeting us, or something in the oven. The result was we all had, or have, rather large appetites. Kids today must miss a mother being there to greet them.

From Miss MacKinlay to Miss Gibson, different, still fair, then Miss Henderson – a memory less strong, possibly a shorter time and less well-liked. Then Mr Kinloch for the top two classes – with hindsight could have been better, but the teaching was still good. Drill was in the playground, consisting of rival games or else exercises indoors when wet.

I had to pass a bursary exam to get the train fare to Helensburgh, and, depending on the mark, went to Clyde Street School or the Hermitage School. I went to the Hermitage, but to do Domestic Science. Of course, with the mother I had, I was good at this, but felt I would have liked differently. Anyway, when I left the Hermitage, Mrs Allan (at the Castle) would have paid for me to go to the "Dough School", but Mother said "No". She was right. I might have felt indebted. I suppose it was Mrs Allan's recommendation that got me a job in Daly's. First year in the Counting House and then four years in corsetry and negligee. They were happy years – mostly.

Must go back a bit. Cathie and Iain are missing from this story. There were over eight years between Cathie and me, six with Iain, and there was before me a sister, Mary, who died at a year and ten months. There is a lovely picture of my parents with that three of a family.

Left to right – Cathie, Mary and Iain

Cathie and Iain both went to Dumbarton Academy for secondary education. Cathie went on to shorthand and typing college in Glasgow for a year. She had a job with Harvey, Chemists, on the front in Helensburgh, but didn't like the confinement. She left and took a job with Miss Anderson, Innestore, Helensburgh, and thereafter stayed in domestic service until she married. She worked in Airth Castle as a housemaid, met Robert Jack, cricketer and violinist, and married him in our parlour at Kilmahew Cottage. Mr Maxwell, our good old minister, officiated. Cameo memory, wonderful the icing that breaks off a tiered iced cake! The house had been busy with visitors beforehand bringing gifts, and busy afterwards sending out cake. Robert was an invalid for years and Cathie worked hard, supported by her parents and the rest of the family. She finally came to stay with Rachel *(in Helensburgh)*. Iain died at 47.

Funnily enough, I do not remember Iain leaving to start work with Nobel's, Falkirk. I suppose he had been travelling to college before that and had his qualification. He was a perfectionist in work, very precise and exacting in most things, but having a great deal of kindness. Through time, and I don't know where, he met Jessie Rennie, a teacher from Lenzie, her aunt from Cardross. Jessie's mother had died earlier and she was married from her aunt's house. At this time Iain was in Westquarter and their new home was in Saltcoats. Donald and I, Innes and Kirsteen had many happy holidays there with them and Isabel, Margaret and Donald.

The two following poems show that similar sacrifices were having to be made for the war effort in the two World Wars.

13

The Old Wooden Horse

They chopped up my wooden horse (my old oak table too!)
The fire was no good,
So they used the wood
To make us all a cup of tea.

The cheese scones were great
The meringues on a plate,
Filled us all with great glee,
God bless the wooden horse (and table of course!)
For helping our afternoon tea.

Don't feel sad sister
Although you may feel mad,
There are worse things happening at sea
Bring out your boat, keep well afloat,
You still have your family, sister Neilina, and me!

Rachel MacInnes

The MacInnes children and their friends chop up another rocking horse and table at Cardross School. Easy Come Easy Go!

Rachel served as a Queen Alexandra's nurse in India during the Second World War.

From Mother to Rachel in India

They took down our aerial tree
And they hauled it to the mill
To make sleepers and poops
And huts for our troops
They took down our aerial tree.

No music for you, Rae, when again you return
Just you hurry home and you'll see,
No programmes from Ireland,
Nothing but silence
Since they took down our aerial tree.

There are others as fine in the field in a line,
But they've no friendly greeting for me.
The one that radiated gladness
Now causes me sadness,
To its memory I'll add R.I.P.

But I'm not alone in my sorrow tonight,
There are others much sadder than me,
The blackbird and thrush,
Which had nests in the bush
At the front of our aerial tree.

PART 2

1. BACKGROUND

(From a lecture given by Margaret to the Historical Society of Sleat, delivered in her late seventies)

The history of a township is not just the recording of the known facts of moneyed and inherited properties, which documents are more easily found, but it is the fabric of the peasantry and the diligence and communication of all strata living there.

The first glimpse we have of the history of Skye is in the poems of Ossian supposed to have composed in the 3rd century.

I am sure you may all find it hard to envisage the days when the Druids were here. It would be easier to picture the Danes and Norwegians, and the Lochlannaich would sometimes shelter in our harbour and sack on shores on their way from Tarskavaig to Kyleakin. The late Dr Murchison said that in his own native Kylerhea they still spoke in his boyhood of a time when from Kyleakin to the Point of Sleat, a distance of 30 to 40 miles, the trees were so thick that, if you put a white horse in at one end, it could not be seen again until it emerged at the other end. All these trees were burned down and the charred stumps sometimes met us when we cut our peats. (You may think the white horse fanciful, but some months ago my cousin in Torrin had to have the forester find some of his cattle which had strayed into the woods at Corrie.)

There is a lasting impact of the Vikings on our people, apart from the obvious legacies such as place names. The long prose tale is characteristic of both the Celts and the Norse. Perhaps there is a Norse connection in Martin Martin's statement that "the inhabitants of the Isles are generally well-proportioned and perhaps there is no part of the globe where so few imperfections are to be seen."

16

Let's leave the Lochlannaich and meet with Sir Donald Munro, High Dean of the Isles, who travelled this way in 1549. He says, "At the west side of Skye lies an island called Oransay, ane myle lange, inhabit and manuit quid land pertaining to Donald Gormsome."

And Martin Martin tells us in 1695 that – "Island Oransa which is a peninsula at low tide is a mile in circumference and very fruitful in corn and grass – the best grass in the area! The main high tides are 10th September and $10 – 20^{th}$ March. Some of the natives are dexterous in engraving trees, birds, deer, dogs etc upon bone, horn or wood with only a sharp-pointed knife. Several of both sexes have quick vein of poesy. It is a general observation of all such as live by the sea coast that they are more prolific than any other people whatsoever."

Isle Ornsay

I have always been interested in the early story of Camuscross, but it is difficult to unearth facts. Camus-na-croise, the bay of the cross, was said to have a chapel there and a nunnery on the island. There is, of course, the remains of the chapel on the island. Beyond Duisdale there is Leitir Chaillich – the nuns' half-land, or piece of land. Forbes, in his place names, 1923, says this was a centre of monastic institutes of yore. Perhaps all records were lost at the time of the Reformation. Eigg was quite a centre of Catholicism earlier and I feel there must have been a strong linking between the two areas.

In 1777 John MacInnes owned Kinloch and his son, Donald, had Camuscross and Duisdale as one farm about 1800.

Back to Isleornsay – From Fraser Macintosh's Antiquarian notes of 1565 he writes of Teampull Oransay at the end of a large tidal island, 100 yards from, and 40 feet above, the high water mark. Signs of an old burial ground with the remains of an old church, 26 and a half feet in length and 13 and a half feet in breadth internally. The walls were built of stone and it had a shell and lime door on the west side.

There is little sign of the wall today. There is a burial ground there which was earlier used by the people during a severe outbreak of smallpox well over a century ago in Camuscross and the bodies were ferried out on a raft for burial. Some of my forebears were buried there. Bella MacDonald recounted a story, told to her by Bella Robertson's father, of the time he went to his uncle's – John Maclean's – funeral in Kylerhea. It was dark when their boat arrived at Glenelg and, not knowing the Porter's house, they tried in vain for shelter. As they knocked at the doors, each light was extinguished and they had to sleep behind a hay-stack. They joined the mourners in Kylerhea the following morning and came back in convoy to the island burying place. (The Glenelg folk must have thought they were Skye raiders!) I think the eradication of smallpox was one of the great achievements of this century.

It was also interesting to read in the Ordnance Gazetteer 1903 that the depth of the sea at the entrance to Loch Hourne is 50 fathoms below the surrounding sea bottom, which has a depth of 60 fathoms, but the depression gradually diminishes to 20 fathoms as the hollow extends south westwards. In several of these depressions, groups of shells of Arctic habitat still linger, survivals of those that lived in British Seas in the glacial epoch. Further on it says that close to the mouth of Loch na Dal is Isleornsay, small but well-sheltered. "The wind strikes down on ye like the blows of a hammer right left ahint before straight down on your head right up under your nose, coming from the Lord kens where, though the sea be smooth as my cheek. I mind o'seeing a brig (it – the wind) carry away her topmast and tear her foresail like a rag. I've seen the day when fishing boats running out of the wee harbour there would be taking their sails off and on twenty times in as many minutes. Many the lives have been lost off Skye with the wind from the hills."

Let us skip quickly over the trials of our people here in the wake of Culloden. Military service ceased, the rents of the tacksmen were increased and therefore of the crofter. There was peace but no security and many emigrated to the Brave New World. This began in the 1770's and travellers to the Highlands like Dr Johnson made their report of the "epidemical fury of emigration." The Highland problem started then, and to stem the flow of people to Cape Breton and the Gulf of the St Lawrence new projects were started like the Caledonian Canal in 1803. The kelp industry boomed, then dropped, herring fishing was irregular and prices for the black cattle rose and fell. In Skye they had two major periods of potato blight, with much privation in 1847, but no deaths.

The horror and devastation of the Clearances, the enforced deportation of the people, and the makeshift homes in Duisdale and Cruard, and at last the uprising of the crofters and the visitation here of the Government Royal Commission for the Napier Report on the 17th May 1883. At the time of the Napier Report the tacksmen named in Sleat were Mr MacDonald, Ord, Mr MacDonald of Tormore and Gillen, Mr Kennedy of the shop, Kennedy & Co, Isleornsay, who also had Kinloch.

Witnesses said there was doubt about who was in business with Kennedy, perhaps MacPherson, the factor, who had given three houses to MacPhersons who were outsiders, and who had also taken Calum MacPherson's house from him for one of these new people. Allan Campbell, crofter, Teangue, said there were now 17 families living where there used to be 8.

John Martin, aged 60, crofter and catechist in the Church of Scotland – Donald MacKinnon's maternal grandfather – said to the Commission,

"People go to work all over because the crofts are too small."

Asked what the wages were, he replied,
"£5 - £8 for a period of 3 – 5 months."
He also said there was more schooling among the young people and they
read newspapers.
"How old is the township? (Teangue)"

"People say it was formed 60 years ago, but there were a few living in it
before then, but then it wasn't partitioned into lots."

"Where did the people come from?"

"From all quarters. Those anxious to get land just came and squatted, but it
was dangerous for the livestock and far to go for peat which had to be
brought home in creels on their backs."

Rev Finlay Graham, Free Church minister and Rev Cameron, parish minister
both testified against the system and helped parishioners prepare
documents. Rev Graham spoke out against the Poor Law inspector now
resident in Portree and carrying out other duties, such as road inspector etc
and not assisting the paupers in Sleat. Donald MacInnes (aged 70), crofter,
Duisdale said Mr MacDonald, Tormore had made the township to give to the
people. In the same Ordnance Gazetteer, 1903, I read that Portree, with a
population of 1003, is the only town. The villages are Kyleakin, Isle Ornsay
and Uig. No mention of Broadford!

The lighthouse was built in 1851 costing £4,527. One man was killed while working there and is buried on the island. My Grandmother from no. 40 was the first woman to sign the visitors' book. This book was later taken to Edinburgh when the lighthouse became automatic. There were two cottages built for shift workers, which were acquired eventually by Gavin Maxwell, but later sold when he went to Camusfearna on the Glenelg side. At present it is untenanted and on the market. The lighthouse has worked well with its present means of lighting since I was a child, and if, at the moment, it has to be served with electricity, I think that the 1985 method is underground cabling. As I understand it, the difference in cost would not be sufficient

reason to despoil what is our birth right and should be readily absorbed by the Lighthouse Commission and the Northern Electricity Board.
(The cabling did in fact, not go underground, but an effort may have been made to minimise the effect as, standing on my mother's doorstep at Ailsa, one could actually only see one telegraph pole, the others being aligned behind it.)

The "view" from Ailsa, 1 Camuscross

2. Local Business

In the Isleornsay Hotel was John Nicolson, whose wife was Marion Macintyre – her brother, Dugald Macintyre, was at Kinloch Farm. John Nicolson died in 1886 and his family, Flora, Marion and Archie carried on the business. Miss Flora Nicolson was a character and many good stories are told of her. Archie was married to Miss Smith from Lewis, who had been a teacher in Drumfearn, Glenelg and, later, in Duisdale. They had three of a family and Archie carried on in the hotel business. The hotel later came back to Lord MacDonald. In a guide book of the early 1930's, prices are shown as:-

Bed & Breakfast	14/6
Lunch	3/6
Tea	2/-
Dinner	5/-
Boarding	126/- a week

The shop is round the corner and very recently I read on a headstone "in memory of Duncan MacInnes, merchant, Isleornsay, died 1832, aged 54". After that I think it would be Kennedy & Co. My grandmother's uncle, Donald Kennedy, who lived below Cnoc Olaig with his wife, Eliza, worked in the shop. On the 1851 census, he is designated "general shopman", aged 52 years. Following that would be the Elders, father of Colin Elder who rented Knock Farm, shown on the 1853 rent list as being for £400. (The said Colin Elder gave evidence before a select committee of the House of Commons in 1847, stating that the Free Church in Sleat numbered 300 souls). In "The Men of Skye" Am Buth is called one of the oldest commercial establishments in Skye. Going to Isleornsay to buy tea became a catchword in the district. After that the shop was the Grahams', then John MacDonald's, Iain a' bhuth, who was joined later by his sister and her husband. In my young days, I remember Richard Woodward, a dapper, pleasant, breezy Englishman in the shop. John MacDonald was Alasdair's father and my cousin, Iain MacKenzie, had a high regard for him. He gave him his first lamb when he was a schoolboy.

Where the Talla Dearg is today was the salt store and above it the meal store, with Lachlan a Meanaig, Lachlan Maclean, working there around 1900 and Seoras MacKay in the shop. The MacKays lived in the house where the wee shop is today. It was a fully stocked shop – all groceries, boots, shoes, pails, jewellery and the big bread hampers from Glasgow standing in the middle of the floor, the bread unwrapped. How did we survive?!

Charlie MacPherson   delivering bread

At that time, the bread and goods would come by the Claymore and the ferrymen, Donald Macpherson and John Beaton, would bring the goods ashore to Isleornsay pier. Of course, the earlier shop in Isleornsay was extremely busy, the people coming from Glenelg and all the places. What a change road transport has brought us!

My paternal grandmother was a sister of Iain a' Chubair, their being kept very busy, as Isleornsay was the port for the herring fleet, the gutting also being done here, with workers coming from the east coast in their own boats. There was quite an export trade of large and small barrels of salt herring – even to Russia. The Manx and Irish fishing fleets passed here on their way to the Shetland fishing. Sometimes the cured herring were shipped by MacBrayne's boats, the Claymore and the Clansman, and sometimes by a special boat. I know that boats from this area went to the Irish coast to fish. I know that my father, when little more than a boy, had a trip on his uncle's boat, fishing off Ireland.

Beautiful steam yachts and sailing ships came into the harbour in the mid-twenties and of course fishing boats passed up and down the channel, but there was no convergence of herring boats as there had been in my grandfather's day, when it was said you could walk from one side of the bay to the other, from boat to boat. When my husband was a boy in Camuscross,

24

his Uncle Donald, the ferryman, Charlie MacPherson's father, had a boat and there was much fishing, going out to the banks and sometimes to Kylerhea, where on one occasion they were storm-stayed for two nights. Peggy MacColl was reminding me of the time my Donald and her Jack, as schoolboys, were so engrossed with their fishing on a rock in Camuscross Bay that they had to be rescued by boat. Local herring boats used to come into Camuscross Bay when I was a girl and you could have a bucket of herring for one shilling.

At the end of the shop was the Post Office, owned around 1900 by Mrs Anderson, who lived in Tigh a'Choillich, now the hotel annexe. There was a fire in the Post Office and it removed to Duisdale with Mr John Fraser. There my cousin, Mary Robertson (nee MacKenzie) was given her training by Mr Fraser, Mairi and Jetta's father, in the mid-twenties. The Telegram Boy was Andrew Payne, the previous one being Archie MacPherson, my Donald's cousin, and the next one was my own cousin, Iain MacKenzie. All of these went on to the wider world of the GPO. It was in the days of Morse equipment and my cousin, Mary, may tell you of her Gaelic conversations with Kaid Maclean, Mary B's brother and Professor Stewart's uncle, in the Glasgow office. These clerks and telegram boys were lucky. Mrs Fraser's house was joined on – no, the other way around – and cups of tea were plentiful. Previous to the mails being brought by steamer from Stromeferry to Portree, the mail was ferried from Balmacara to Kyleakin and horse-drawn to Portree.

In 1893 the extension of the Highland Railway to Kyle was begun and this was a source of employment. Sir Murdoch MacDonald, MP for many years in Inverness-shire, was in the Civil Engineers office at that time. Until then, and for a good many years afterwards, the ferry was operated by rowing boat, the MacDonald estates claiming the ferry rights. The Kyle railway opened in 1897 and the Mallaig line in 1901.

It was 1807 before road-making began in Skye and it must have been around 1900 that my Grandmother's cousin, Donald Anderson from Duisdale Beag, was given £100 for making the road to Camuscross. His tools were barrow, pick and spade. When the road was planned, it was intended that it should go in front of the houses, but several of the crofters at the near end would not give up their land and there is a song which tells of Peggy and Liza taking up the marking pegs. I think it has been regretted ever since that it did not go that way.

3. The Carers

Along from the shop, where *(the late)* Iain Noble's house now is, was a lovely stone house. In one half lived the shop people, the Grahams, and in the other, the doctor. The first doctor recorded there was Dr Graham, brother of the shopkeeper – he gave evidence for the Napier Report. Around 1890 one doctor served Strath and Sleat and was stationed in Isleornsay. He went on his rounds either by bicycle or horse-drawn trap. There was no telephone. If the doctor was needed, a horse and trap had to be sent for him. There was no district nurse and no hospital. During that time there was an epidemic of scarlet fever, and, although the doctor was attentive under the circumstances, several infants died. There followed Dr Beag Ruadh MacDonald, who strongly recommended a gruel of oatmeal. Then followed Dr Hastings (from Arran?). I liked Bella MacDonald's story of waylaying the Doctor because she had severe toothache. It was raining. She was near the Humpy Bridge. He took her below and pulled the tooth. Haven't we become soft!

My husband's mother broke her leg in her 80's and Dr Hastings set it. A bucket of stones was suspended from the foot over the edge of the bed and this was lightened at intervals to continue the healing process. Some months later, Dr Hastings, coming upon her suddenly, had to warn her to be careful as she scrambled quite briskly up the bank at the back of her house. His earlier treatment must have been successful! With Dr Hastings came Skye's first motor car, but, sadly, the doctor was killed in it in 1918 at the bridge at Knock.

Dr Pretzill followed and went to live in Creag a' Cheann, a house bought by public subscription in Armadale. Some three years later Dr McCall was there, of Liosmor background, and whose family were in Armadale Farm, followed by Dr MacInnes for a few years and then Dr Campbell who was, I'm sure, over thirty years in Sleat, and in thirty years or so someone will tell many stories of Dr Campbell. There was Nurse MacInnes in Dr Hastings time, and also Nurses Ross, Nicol and MacLure. Nurse Cathie Gillies and Nurse Beaton worked with Dr Campbell and were held in the same high regard as he. The earlier nurses covered many miles on foot and on bicycle, and Nurse Beaton was probably the first nurse to have a car. I think it would be in 1927 that my cousin, Mary, and I went round all the houses in Camuscross, Isleornsay and Duisdale and collected 1/- from each for the District Nursing Association.

Of course before these trained nurses came to the parish, maternity cases were attended by local women, some good, some less so. My mother, without training and without her seeking it, provided this service. Helen Roy (1811 – 1875) in no. 39 also provided this service, and quite a number here well- knew the name, Mrs Cook, who lived in no. 11, as the last midwife remembered here. Her son was the Rev William Gillies, Kenmore. It wasn't surprising that in such an outlying area the doctor would arrive too late to help, and I'm afraid that infant mortality was very high.

4. LANDOWNERS

Duisdale House

DUISDALE HOUSE/ MacKINNON

The first occupants of Duisdale House, which was built for them, were Miss Flora MacKinnon and her sister and brother. They were of the well-known MacKinnon family of Kilbride, Corry, Kyleakin. Miss Florrie, as she was known, must have been the oldest member of the family, or the dominant one – when she wanted work done on a good day, the crofters had to leave theirs and do it. Peggy MacColl tells me that Jack's grandfather and grand uncle had no option but to leave their houses in Duisdale when that ground was wanted for Duisdale House. They were housed in adjacent crofts in Camuscross, and it is in Jack's Aunt Eliza's croft that Rae and Peggy live. Iain and Connie MacInnes and their father now live in the other one. I expect that eviction would be around 1860. The rent records of 1873/74 show James Grant had been moved from 4 to 5 Duisdale, leaving the block 1-4 to the MacKinnons and around 1890, 1 – 3 were cleared for Duisdale House.

Miss Florrie had another side to her nature. About 1885 she passed a group of people worshipping in the open – the school was not available then – and she organised the collecting of money, and herself gave the major

28

contribution, for the building of St Columba Church in Duisdale. It is a beautiful church in a beautiful spot. After Miss Florrie died, Duisdale House lay empty for some years. Then Lachlan MacKInnon and his wife came from Melbourne, Australia and hoped that their son would stay, but he did not. It was let for some years to the Patons, and the late Bella MacDonald and other local people enjoyed their work there. Bella would go down to London, travelling first class with them. Duisdale later went to the MacDonalds and then was let to Iain MacLeod.

Newspaper cutting

ISLEORNSAY – The Duisdale and Drumfearn scholars, together with some of the parents, were this year again entertained to a splendid treat, generously provided by Mr Lachlan MacKinnon, of Duisdale. Though now resident in Melbourne, Australia, he has not forgotten the children dwelling in the vicinity of his beautiful Highland home, nor limited his generosity of former years. The catering arrangements were placed with Mr and Mrs Nicolson, the Schoolhouse, Duisdale, assisted by young ladies of the district. An amusing feature was the Highland stories related by the pupils, Mairi Fraser, Annie MacLennan and Mary Robertson. Highland music was rendered on the gramophone operated by Miss MacKinnon, Camuscross. The Hon. Iona MacDonald represented Mr MacKinnon, and at the conclusion handed each pupil a gift of 5/-, cake, fruit, sweets and chocolate. Mr Nicolson referred to the loss sustained by Sleat in the death of the Hon. Mrs Godfrey MacDonald, Ostaig, who in previous years never failed to be present, contributing by her grace and charm to the success of the gathering. He impressed on the children the gratitude due to Mr MacKinnon for this annual treat, and called for hearty cheers to Mr and Mrs MacKinnon and their son, and also for the Hon. Iona MacDonald and to those who helped to make the entertainment a success.

MacDONALD

<u>Newspaper cutting</u>

BANQUET AT ARMADALE CASTLE, SKYE 1919

For 13th January (the old style New Year's Day), Lady MacDonald of the Isles invited all the men of Sleat who had returned from the late War, after service by sea and land. Some 40 assembled, an equal number being absent in the South and a similar number having perished. All the family and many neighbours were present to honour the guests and assist in serving the bounteous repast spread at sunset on the brilliantly-lighted tables in the dining-room, decorated with plate and trophies and flowers. Seats at the head of the table were placed for the boys of the late Hon. Godfrey MacDonald as the hosts of the gathering, Masters Alasdair and Seumas. A blessing was asked by the Rev. Kenneth Ross, parish minister, and at the close of the repast the toast list was carried through.
Colonel Martin, Ostaig, gave "The King", referring to the value of the Royal Authority as the only link binding us with our outer Dominions, and

mentioning that the lack of our old established institutions prevented the American people from participating in the recent signing of the Peace protocol, as it found them unprepared and disunited in an unforeseen crisis. Rev. K. Ross proposed the health of Lady MacDonald, whose many sufferings and bereavements had not diminished her constant solicitude and affection for those around her.

Mr Loyd, Tormore, proposed the guests of the evening and alluded to the long and unexampled trials they had borne, the heroism they had displayed, and the delight with which the survivors had been received on their return home.

Colonel Kemble replied on behalf of all who had served, and alluded to the tasks of reconstruction which awaited their services on return.

Sergeant Charles Angus proposed the memory of those who had been lost, and this toast was drunk in silence. Thereafter song was varied by recitation, and several duets were rendered by the Hon. Iona MacDonald (piano) and Miss Leila Willoughby (violin), while Mrs Campbell, Camp Rock, Mr John MacLeod and a large proportion of the guests gave an excellent account of themselves. The cook (Miss Jessie MacPherson) and the staff of the Castle also received an ovation which was obviously merited, and their healths were included with that of Mr Ross, the Castle piper, who played excellently at intervals.

Finally "Auld Lang Syne" was sung by all present with hands joined, and after the singing of the National Anthem the company dispersed at a late hour, after an unforgettable evening.

(In somewhat more recent times at Armadale, the editor fondly remembers Bella MacDonald of the tooth extraction story, and childhood visits to Armadale Castle, where Bella was housekeeper – and what she did "keep" was in fact the whole "house". The MacDonalds had, by then, moved out of the castle, a beautiful grand edifice, with a double staircase with a glorious stained-glass window of Somerled, Lord of the Isles, on the half-landing, and a grand banqueting hall with all sorts of treasures on the walls and mantelpieces. Bella lived there alone for close on twenty years, and looked

after it with loving care, airing pillow slips and removing large books from the library shelves to dust them. She would think nothing of walking up the long tree-lined driveway after a whist drive in the pitch dark at 10.30pm, and letting herself in with a huge latch-key, then clicking along the stone corridors with her torch, until she could light a Tilley lamp. Or perhaps coming downstairs from her first-floor bedroom having awakened in the middle of the night, to take just another few from the box of chocolates which she had been given, and was going to deny herself by leaving them out of reach. She had a hearty laugh, a huge loyalty, nerves of steel - and essentially a strong faith.)

MacINNES
There is a story that a family of MacInnes's with seven sons was evicted after felling a large, ancient tree about Leitir-fura, along the shore from Kinloch Lodge. I'm sure the Country Commission would endorse that! Flora MacGillivray, from her husband, John, has a different story – it was said that they owned Kinloch, and a son owned Camuscross and Duisdale. From Donald came the Gobha or blacksmith in Isleornsay, the smithy being where John Henman's house is now. Donald, the Gobha, had a brother, Malcolm, whose son, John, was a general in India, and he had two sons – one Sir Myles MacInnes, MP for Carlisle and the other the Bishop of Jerusalem. So there! I'm merely stating facts. I won't bore you with the wider ramifications.

INA

(Ina Skinner was one of Margaret's closest friends, both through the Skye connection and their life in Glasgow. Ina's father was in service at Armadale Castle).

Ina's father was George Romanes MacKay and was originally from Cromarty. The Romanes were a wealthy family who lived in Cromarty and wanted to adopt George, but George's mother would not allow it. His mother died when he was young and, when he was 15 or 16, the Countess of Cromarty's daughter, Louisa, married Lord MacDonald, and took George to Armadale as kennel-boy, under a keeper who was an Englishman – a hard task-master, but a good teacher. George lived in a bothy at the low stables and was up at 4am. He reared pheasants, trained dogs and all the "hunting, shooting and fishing". He went to Simeer Lodge with a tenant and from there to Duisdale with Miss Flora MacKinnon, who was usually ill-spoken of, but George got on well with her. In Duisdale, he stayed in the cottage below the road, his father with him for part of the time, but the father returned to Cromarty.

George married Catherine Grant, around 1900 and went to Portree to live in a rose-covered cottage in the Lodge near the Cuillin Hills Hotel. Ina, as a young girl, remembers her mother with a tray of sponge cakes cooling, as she was expecting the Misses Fraser, sisters of Lord MacDonald's factor, George Fraser. George Fraser was a life-long friend of George MacKay and the Rev Norman MacLeod, the parish minister, was a regular visitor in Portree. Mrs Mackinnon, the baker's wife was a friend. The MacKinnons had 21 children, doctors, teachers etc and Ina went to school with the grandchildren.

Ina's mother took ill and went to Strathpeffer when Ina was about three. She remembered visiting her there. Mother returned to Portree and the family lived in a flat above the stables. Ina remembered double-opening windows in her bedroom. Ina's mother died and father's niece, Annie, came to stay with him, although Ina went to stay with her Aunt Christina at the Buchanan Retreat in Bearsden in Glasgow. Ina felt strange at the Retreat and was not particularly happy there. She was sent to a private school, "a school for young ladies", run by seven sisters, where samplers and ladylike arts were the order of the day, but Ina hated it – a country girl among snobs. Her father found out and wrote to Auntie that Ina was a girl who would need to earn her living and should go to an ordinary school.

She then had a spell at Bearsden Primary School, with Miss Harvey an excellent headmistress. She later returned to Skye to school at Portree – the headmaster Mr Gillanders. The pupils feared him, but adored his daughter, Muriel Gillanders, who also taught at the school. While she was at Portree School, there was an outbreak of diphtheria and many school children were affected. Ina took it when the outbreak was almost all over and she was the only one in the "fever hospital" at the time. One of her visitors at the window to gaze on her was little Albert Bradley, son of the C. O. at the Drill Hall.

When she was ten, Ina went to Armadale to stay and Albert went with his parents to London. Ina, under her Aunt's direction, corresponded with Albert and later directly with him, until, when at school in Bearsden, a telegram arrived from Albert to say that he was arriving the following day. He arrived, tall and splendid in the Scots Guard uniform, and found slim, dark, red-cheeked Ina had grown into a plumpish girl, dressed most unbecomingly in her cousin, Edith's, cast-offs. He had bought a couple of seats for the King's Theatre, but Auntie had him buy a third and sent Ina's cousin, Kitty, as chaperone. This in no way spoiled Ina's enjoyment. She loved the visit to the theatre, hated her appearance, but enjoyed telling her friends at school of her visitor. Leave was up at the end of the week to the relief of both parties.

At Armadale, Ina remembered the Lady MacDonald holding a ball and the Hon Iona coming to the kennels to learn dancing from Ina's father. Ina viewed the ball from the top of the staircase. The Hon Iona wore a red dress with a Dutch collar in white. She had black hair and was very pretty and attractive. Later Ina visited Iona in Portree House as the Hon Mrs Norman Maclean. Lady MacDonald herself was almost unapproachable, but she did consult George, Ina's father. The castle was let in summer to all sorts of grand people. Ina remembers Earl Spencer there at one stage. There were dances in the evenings and Ina would come to view the spectacle from the foot of the lawns.
Ina went on to teach in Airor and Rhum, before marrying Walter Skinner and coming to Glasgow.

Knock Free Church

5. The Church

My grandmother was a stalwart of the Free Church – her parents must have come out at the time of the disruption. She was born in 1840, but read religious books in Gaelic and English. She had a family Bible reading every morning and evening and, after placing her large Bible on the dresser, went into her bedroom to pray. She always prayed privately. There was a very strict Sunday observance here in both Free Church and Church of Scotland households. We as children relieved that by playing at Sunday schools. In my childhood, all Sunday work was still done on a Saturday and the water was carried from the well in readiness. There were two wells, the top one clear and sparkling – it's still there – and the lower one for the cattle.

In my early teens, I recollect our walk over the hill above the burn to the road, changing our footwear before leaving the moor. On a boggy bit down in a hollow, we saw there the largest, colourful dragonflies. We walked on to Knock to church – three and a half miles in all. The precentor sat in front of my Aunt Rachel's pew and I can still see his very freckled face. In a box on the left sat the Ord girls, the Nicolsons, with their becoming straw hats. Mr MacDonald was a very emphatic preacher.

I remember a communion service when I was around 15, which started at 12 noon. I went in to the English (service) in the hall and at 1 o'clock or so, directly into the Gaelic service in the church, which came out at 3.35. My cousin Mary and I joined the young people in a house not far from the church, enjoying the freedom, the welcome food and tea. The lady of the house was Kirsty Mhor na h-Ardaich, over 80, but young in spirit. My aunt went across the road into Kirsty Buchanan's. Prayer meetings were held each week in different households, Mr MacLure, the missionary, coming from Teangue. I always thought he had a face in which one could see the look of a man at peace with himself and with his God.

I think, looking back, the most tedious meetings were in the schoolhouse, where the elders took turns to pray. Some of them forgot to stop and of course we were standing. For the young girls things were brightened somewhat by the row of young men lumped together at the back.

6. SCHOOLING

My grandmother, Mary Kennedy, was born in 1840 and lived in Cnoc Ollaig. She went to the General Assembly Agricultural School, which was at the side of Phemie Anderson's house. She was taught by Alasdair Nicolson — "schoolmaster, session clerk and registrar" in the 1875 census. On the 1853 rent roll, the rent of £3.16/- was paid by Lady MacDonald. There was a similar school in Tormore. My grandmother could read and write in both Gaelic and English, and, I'm given to understand, was versed in theology.
My mother, born in 1879, with her older sisters and younger one, went to Duisdale School which must have opened in the 1880's.There were around ninety pupils at that time. If my memory is right, my mother's teacher was Mr McCully from Orkney, typical of his time, no Gaelic spoken in school, but from the later correspondence that went on between the sisters, he must have been a good teacher. Before or after him, the teacher was Mr Copland.

My husband, Donald Grant, born 1903, grew up in 29 Camuscross, his grandfather having been a shepherd at Kinloch. I would say those of his time were lucky in education. They had Mr MacLeod, Jane Nicolson's father and then Mr MacKinnon, who later became a minister, and both were native Gaelic speakers with Skye background. In Donald's time the pupils numbered around 40, decreasing to around 26 in 1920.

Donald, my husband, went to Portree (Secondary) School, the only lad from here at the time. Christina Macdonald and Ann Beaton from Tarskavaig were also there then. There were, of course, no hostels, and he lodged with a family who kept three students. They would take what food they could from home - eggs, meal, potatoes etc. At the weekend each would buy his own piece of mutton which would be cooked in the large soup pot, with an identifying piece of thread on each. Their usual way to travel was to walk to Broadford and get the steamer from there to Portree. (Which reminds me, Broadford Pier was erected by the Fishery Board in 1892 at a cost of £10,000, through the aid of a loan from Lord MacDonald.)

Donald went on to Glasgow University, had the small Carnegie Grant, worked all his holidays, each summer, as pantry man in one of the Clyde steamers. His father had died when he was three; his mother when he was sixteen. He, and others like him, had to make their way with little help. I won't give you my opinion on present day student grants. His brother, Angus, older on returning from war service and injured, finished his course and taught for some time in Ferindonald.

Education was important. Those who hadn't been able to have it wanted their families educated, and there were also those who wanted to learn.

Letter to the Oban Times, January 14, 1947, written by John MacGillivray, Maryburgh, Ross-shire, but belonging to Camuscross and later again resident there. It was regarding correspondence about Lt-Col. John MacInnes, author of "The Brave Sons of Skye", published in 1899.

"Lt.-Col, John MacInnes was born in Sasaig, Sleat, a township midway between the villages of Isleornsay and Ardvasar. On completing his primary education in the local school, John MacInnes, and another lad, John MacKinnon, Camuscross, received their secondary education in the parish manse of Sleat, to which they resorted three days a week for two years. John MacInnes's home was two miles from the Manse, and John MacKinnon's five miles.

These lads were taught all subjects necessary to enable them to enter the Training College, by the very worthy minister, Rev. John Forbes, who was parish minister of Sleat from 1851 to 1863.

John MacInnes became schoolmaster at Benderloch and thereafter at Glendarroch until he retired in 1909.

John MacKinnon, like his companion, completed his course with distinction at the Training College, became headmaster at Erbusaig, Lochalsh, and thereafter at Breakish, Broadford, Skye, where, after many years of excellent work, he was compelled, through ill-health, to give up his profession and retire to Cruard, Isleornsay, where he built a house which he shared with his widowed sister, Janet, and her family, her husband having been drowned at sea."

Archie Campbell, Shiloh, Breakish, is a great grandson of Janet and their family history makes interesting reading.

7. HOUSING

The price of wood was prohibitive in Skye – that is why so much zinc and corrugated iron was used. The Crofting Commission heard many appeals for restitution for the beams burned down at the time of the Clearances. The house we bought, Ailsa, 1 Camuscross, was a pre-fabricated building brought from Greenock some 80 years ago. A snug, compact home. The Gillies's had moved in from Sasaig. There was a big corrugated iron shed built on at the end and Mrs Gillies had a thriving laundry business there. Her husband was a tailor and used his boat on his trips to measure and fit his clients. Their son was a banker in Greenock, their daughter, Maggie, a teacher in Ferindonald and later in Greenock. Cathie was finally an x-ray sister in a Glasgow hospital, after spending some years as a district nurse in Sleat.

In 1851 Camuscross had 50 houses, including 10 in Cruard and 3 in Baravaig and by 1871 this had altered to 54 houses, including 10 in Cruard and only 1 in Baravaig. Cruard had tiny lots, called garden grounds, renting at 3/9 a lot, although some had double lots. Listed in Cruard in that year are 2 shoemakers, 2 dressmakers and 1 tailor. Camuscross rents ranged from £1.16/- to £3.3/- and one double one at £5.8/-. In the 1853 list, the rent was paid for no. 40 by my maternal great-great grandfather for his own and his daughter's houses. From my great-great-great grandfather, Donald MacKinnon, our family can count eight generations and the family of Hector MacKenzie is the eighth generation in the direct line to be living in no. 40. It is inherited through the female side as my grandparent's only son was drowned when 21 years. It is interesting to read all the trades on the census returns – cooper, blacksmith, crofters, labourers, farmers, dairymaid/man, shipowner, dressmaker, schoolmaster, nurse, catechist.
This one amused me - Mary MacInnes 52 : occupation – "nothing whatever".
This one interesting - Hugh MacKinnon : Chelsea Pensioner 86, Mary, his wife 76, Ann Robertson: house servant. I was glad the old couple had a servant and he a Chelsea Pensioner.

<u>Bits of information about the houses in Camuscross before and in Margaret's retirement time 1970 - 1992</u>

6. Granddaughter, Peggy MacConnell from Glasgow, stayed with grandparents for some time. Her brother, Victor, built a new house on the site at no. 29 Camuscross in the last two years. He has an adult family. Donnie and Colleen MacKinnon, with three children, now in a new house in no. 6.

8. Mrs Flora MacGillivray, in her late husband's home, the rebuilt home of his people.

9. Peggy Nicolson was there, widow of Donald Nicolson, sailor, bard and story-teller but the house is now empty.

10. Donald (H) Mackinnon's old home – he now has new house built over 18 years ago on a neighbouring croft (Mary MacLure's father's croft – MacArthur). Old house, now owned by his sister, lies empty.

12. Katie MacPherson and one grown daughter live there – Willie MacPherson's widow.

15. This is where the Church Agricultural School (later a state school) was around 1850, which was the school my Grandmother attended. My mother went to Duisdale School.

16. Bella MacDonald's old home. ("Bella the Castle" worked for many years for Lord MacDonald and lived for many years alone in Armadale Castle, which she looked after with loving care). Home sold to an artist. Farquhar MacLennan and his family live there.

24. Owned by Mr & Mrs Pat Walsh. New chalet built on same croft. They also own 31, their initial purchase.

25. Mrs MacColl and Rae live there now. Jack and Peggy, on retirement, had new house built there some eight years ago, on the site of his aunt's and his own home.

32. Mr & Mrs Angus Campbell, in the early twenties, had three boarded-out children from Glasgow – Maggie, Tommy and Bella MacColl. The two younger ones went elsewhere as the Campbells were old, but Maggie stayed through school and was a great help to them then and later.

33. Mr & Mrs Neil Kennedy. Older when married. Had two superior boarded-out boys from Glasgow, Andrew and James Payne. Andrew won Gaelic prize at Duisdale School. On leaving school, he went to Duisdale to the Post Office with Mr Hugh Fraser (Isleornsay P O, but situated in Duisdale). From there he progressed to responsible positions down south, returning later to Kyle. James emigrated with a batch of teenagers to a family in Canada, and he, and some of the others of that lot, were never heard of again.

35. This house was built for my Aunt Christina, my mother's sister, when she married Neil MacKinnon, an uncle of Donald (H) Mackinnon. A few years later they emigrated to the USA. Mr & Mrs Donald Edwards there now. Mary Bell (Mrs Edwards) was there with her granny in 1926.

36. This house, now a ruin, had belonged to MacKinnons from Elgol; their family was there in my mother's time. My cousin, Mary, from 40, remembers being told of the son, John, who became a famous artist in Australia.

37. My father was born in this house, his mother coming over from Airor, Knoydart to have her second baby. This was her home. She was a MacKinnon. Her family were coopers to trade.

39. The original house here would be built around 1835 for my great-great grandfather's daughter as he paid the rent for both crofts in the 1851 rent list. She married Robert Roy, a soldier. Looking some years back at the byre in 39, good stone walls, I think this would be the original house and later the newer house would be built – it is rather close to no. 40.

No 40 and no 39

40. My mother's home. My grandfather died in 1903, my grandmother in 1925. Aunt Rachel (Mrs MacKenzie), the eldest daughter, was at home there with her family. They came home initially for health reasons for one of the

family, but could not leave the grandmother. The children all had their schooling in Duisdale School. Their father died in 1923. In 1926 Alex, the eldest, was at sea, Mary in the Post Office with Mr Fraser in Duisdale – Andrew Payne was the telegram boy there then, the postman being Ivy Macdonald and Iain Anderson was the Tarskavaig postman, taking all the mails by horse and trap. Iain MacKenzie, Rachel's younger boy, after another year at school, got Andrew Payne's job and completed his career in Paisley, from which he retired in 1972. Unable to find a croft in Camuscross, he found one in Torrin. Alex, the older son, after being at sea, joined the police in Greenock and then, with Molly his wife, retired to no. 40 Camuscross. After his death in 1970, the house was closed, except for holidays.

Five years ago, his son, Hector, retired from the police and his youngest offspring, Heather, is in her 5th year in Portree High School. Graham, her older brother, after taking his qualification in Inverness, works in Strathaird fish farm. The eldest works outwith Skye. Heather is the eighth generation in direct line living in no 40.

The 3 sisters left in this country

Maggie, Liza and Rachel
Christina emigrated to the USA

8. PEOPLE

Some of those who made their mark towards the end of the last century and the beginning of this.

General MacInnes, son of Miles MacInnes of Cnoc Nollaig, and the General's sons, Sir Miles MacInnes, M.P. for Carlisle, and his brother, Bishop of Jerusalem.

Lt.-Col. John MacInnes, author of "The Brave Sons of Skye" – see under "education".

James Kennedy, town clerk of Greenock, who spoke 7 languages, the basic one being his native Gaelic.

John MacKinnon, from 36 Camuscross, who became a well-known artist in Australia.

I liked the story of Archie Campbell's brother, John, who around 1900 owned the Bradbury Hotel in North Berwick which had separate suites and sometimes foreign royalty and their staffs stayed there.

And later, Bella's father, Captain Robertson, who received his decoration for cable-laying in deep Australian waters.

Also Mrs Margaret MacNiven for work in the prison service.

And Hugh Millar spent some time in Isleornsay – but that is another story.

Then we have the many who went into service. How we, in our language, have altered and denigrated the word service. One can serve without being servile. We are all serving every day of our lives. Through the years I have met some fine men and women who learned well their own craft, and others at the learning process and these were people of grace and distinction.

I remember attending the 80th birthday party of Christina Nicolson of Duisdale, whose father was the mail carrier, using a pony and trap, from Isleornsay to Broadford around 1890. She was a woman who had much to teach.

I remember Christina MacPherson of 36? Camuscross, married for a short time to Robertson from Cruard and making her steady, independent way through life. I met her in Byres Road, in Glasgow, in a little grey suit, pink blouse and navy and pink hat – a figure many a girl would envy – and she 90 years of age. I haven't time to tell any of the funny stories.
(The editor does well remember Christina, in daytime service in Jordanhill, not letting on to her employer that she was quite probably older than they themselves, or when she eventually succumbed to taking a taxi to our house, asking to be put off round the corner so that she could still, in her 90's, walk the last bit to the house.)

I remember Mary MacLure (Mary MacArthur of Camuscross), related to both Donald and myself, her interest and kindness to our children and her wisdom and simplicity.
(Auntie Mary MacLure was the calmest old lady whom I loved visiting in her Partick flat, and passing the time when the adults were talking by counting the cards, pictures, trays and ornaments of cats which everybody sent her – and then counting them in reverse to see if I got the same number! Tommy was the name of her much-petted cat.)

Many can give the names of many others, each remembered by their families and many other people.

My grandmother died in 1925. I remember her daughter, my Aunt Rachel, there at no. 40 with a cow and a calf to feed, and at haymaking having a long way to carry the hay on bundles on her back to the byre. I remember the heartsease, vetch and orchis that grew on the lower stretches of the croft. I rarely see heartsease today.

I remember the fire built outside and the large black cauldron on top, heating – the water all carried from the well – and the clean, white washing that emerged. My aunt was kind and good and not too critical of the young. She was a very hard worker, and, though widowed and with a hard time of it bringing up her family, she still laughed – though quietly.

Donald MacInnes and his sister-in-law, Rachel

Next door, at that time, were Mr & Mrs Campbell, she with a gift for telling stories. She was very kind to us. My cousin, Mary, took all her woes there. At one time, Mary and Mrs Campbell walked to Dalavil with a stirk. Mary remembers a very attractive old lady there, with a white shawl, Morag Hannah's mother. Now you know from where Morag gets her good looks.

9. PERSONAL MEMORIES

I shall try to give quick impressions of my young days on holiday in Skye. Predominantly perhaps the number of old ladies. I'm afraid the dark dress did play a part in the impression, but I remember the kindness of the people, and, if they were very poor, I wasn't aware of it. Certainly they were very plain and workmanlike in dress. Many men were bearded, but only the older ones.

Grand Aunt Mary MacKinnon, 7 Camuscross
Centre – Granny Mary MacKinnon, 40 Camuscross
Right – Mrs Lachlan Campbell, 39 Camuscross

Most kitchens had their dresser, the trusaid? - wooden settee, and in some houses, they had a kist with uprising lid, in which was kept the meal and flour. By the way, these flour bags were put to many uses by the people, who, all of them at that time, would have needed every penny. Bleached, they made excellent pillowslips – it took a lot of elbow grease to erase the name "MacFarlane & Shearer". Good lining for patchwork quilts, and towels of all description.

From a kist, Bean Eachain would bring out a sweetmeat for a girl, something she had hidden from her family. Peggy and Tina lived a few houses apart, but often shared meals and usually shared visitors, the one calling to the other to come and enjoy the company. And they were jolly. And made black-currant jam. Mary Gillies in Cruard, making blackcurrant jam, the currants from her garden, and looking after James and Finlay, and Farquhar Abby coming in there one day and making a never-ending grace. John MacLure, the missionary, with the peace of God written on his face.

And a bit later, when I was fifteen, walking round from no.40 and crossing the moor to meet my cousin, Mary, at the Post Office, the path almost at the door of Bella's home, and one would stop for a moment and say hello to Oidhrig, or a time when Donald Grant was cutting the hay there. Another cameo – Phemie Anderson busy with corn, and her hair in little golden red curls on her face. The burn and the rocky stepping stones a hazard when the burn was in spate. Pick up Mary at the Post Office, perhaps say hello to Tina, and Mairi and Jetta (her daughters) – I always called her Mrs Fraser, but the truly local called her Tina and her husband Mr. Fraser. And call at Johnnie Ivy's, where his mother had a wee shop at the end of the house.

(A digression – that reminds me that Donald, my husband, loved to help his uncle Ewan in this wee shop which was at the house. He (Ewan) was a fish curer and would sell that and all useful groceries. It was no longer there in my time.)
Kate and Johnnie would be there. I don't think these shops could pay – cups of tea were often provided with the service. Mary would sometimes go to Isleornsay from the Post Office, where she was teaching Philip Hamburger. He lived in the old Graham house, which was rather dilapidated, with his mother and they were a bit of a mystery. Later it was said that he was James Robertson Justice. On our way home we would call in at Mrs. MacKinnon's wee shop – the shed still stands where I park and turn my car at Mrs MacGillivray's – and Mary would be there and we might buy sweets, or, if lucky, get one. No profit again!

An interesting chapter in Martin Martin's book tells of nature cures by the use of plants, dulse or sea-ware. When listening to Jimmy Mack's programme the other day, I heard of a new bandage to be put on the market, using seaweed for the control of bleeding and the healing of ulcers etc.

The best dulse soup I have tasted was made from mutton stock with barley and vegetable added, but I'm sure one could make a health-giving bree with dulse and oatmeal. We used to collect carrageen in Barravaig *(just beyond no.40)*, and my mother was an expert in producing a flavoured soup.

There was a spinning-wheel in each home and the women carded or spun. I remember, around 1922 or 3, when I was ten or so, being told that the slime of a snail would cure warts, which I had on two fingers. My cousin, Iain MacKenzie, performed the application, he being quite willing to handle a large, black snail. It worked.

Later in my teens, I remember in 1932 going with May Greenshields, Donald's cousin, to a dance, Donald seeing me home to no. 40, and from then on it was looking forward – and now looking back.

(Margaret kept a copy of two obituaries, published in the Free Church magazine of 15/8/1925. Apart from the co-incidence of their appearing together, it amused her to tell her Donald that the first – and much longer one – was for her Grandmother, while the second somewhat shorter one was for Donald's.)

Mrs Mackinnon, Camuscross, Sleat.

15-8-25

We much regret to have to record the removal of this worthy woman in August last. She was brought to a knowledge of the truth when comparatively young, and to the end of her life she was a most faithful witness in every respect on the side of the Lord. During the days of Mr Roderick Macleod she invariably attended the Snizort Communion, leaving early on Thursday morning and arriving before the beginning of the service after walking every step of the way—a distance of over forty miles. For close on fifty years she was a member of this congregation. A gentle, loving woman, it was most edifying to be in her company and hear her relate the sayings and doings of those excellent ministers and men all gone home to their rest. She has now followed them, having left behind her a beautiful Christian example, and a fragrant memory.

Mention should also be made of one of a similar spirit with her, and who for years had been her near neighbour—Mrs Arch. Macpherson, Camuscross, who passed away some time ago. A humble, affectionate, and God-fearing woman, she was a great favourite among the people. For over forty years a member of this congregation, she, in company with Mrs Mackinnon, often journeyed toward the House of God together; and now, we believe, that they are both enjoying the rest that remaineth for the people of God.   J. M.

I was at the Isleornsay Games in 1936. If I remember rightly, that was their second year and they did not continue. (It has always been difficult here to maintain momentum. For example, we have no community council. Will you all please sign the appeal!). The games were held in the park and where Mary MacInnes's house is now would be the place for the tug o' war.

Ceilidhs' and dances in the Talla Dearg, a very rough, splintery floor. Dr Neil MacLeod, Dr Campbell, Donald Grant and other local worthies in the chair. Charlie MacPherson singing, Mary B (MacLean) giving her readings and Jackie MacPherson with his box. Happy times!

A wee memory here of Mary B in Shorag. My uncle from Wallasey, Donald and me making our way back to no. 40 after listening to Dr Baxter in the wee church. Mary B inviting us in for sherry and my uncle tickled pink – a change from his boyhood in Breakish.

I have quite a reasonable record of the intertwining of families, but it is difficult and time-consuming to delve up the facts with so many families of the same name. It is a long time since I started this ploy, but unfortunately not early enough.

Food was plain, but good. Eggs, milk and butter, crowdie and stapag from the cream. Very tasty Skye mutton from MacAskill, the butcher from Knock Farm and buntata gorm - blue potatoes. These early potatoes were lovely, usually ready for the last Sunday in July, the Communion. Scones and oatcakes and dumpling. All doors were open to one and much kindness shown.

Bella MacDonald (Bella the Castle) who lived where Farquhar MacLennan now lives, used to speak of the times when at full moon of the low tide the muirsgian, or spoutfish, would rise to the surface. A group of them would go to Camuscross Bay to collect them amid much fun and laughter and return to my Grand Aunt Mary's for tea.

10. DONALD GRANT

Perhaps now we've reached Kinloch, I should tell you that my husband's grandfather, also Donald Grant, was a shepherd living in the cottage in the bay beyond the white-washed house. There is only a ruin there now. They usually came across to Isleornsay by boat, I understand. These Grants would originally make their way from Speyside to Glen Urquhart and Invermorriston. There is a poem called "The Curse of Moy", written by J B Morritt, a friend of Sir Walter Scott, which tells of the Grants and Urquharts weighing power against the MacIntoshes in the 14th century. A few people may remember Donald Grant's son, Ewan, who lived in 2 Camuscross. He was a merchant and fish curer. Rachel Gillies married Ewan Grant in Isleornsay Hotel on 1st. June, 1897, his first wife, a MacInnes from Knoydart, having died. Rachel Gillies was the daughter of Mrs Cook, the well-known midwife.

(*My mother kept many newspaper cuttings about my Father, who was a prominent stalwart of everything Highland, and she did give me a very full and special scrapbook of the threads of his life, in photo and newspaper articles. She kept her own thoughts of him very precious, not putting them into writing. She was immensely proud of his numerous achievements – he was crowned Bard of An Comunn Gaidhealach by the Queen Mother, then the Duchess of York, at the 1936 National Mod, he was a shinty "blue" at Glasgow University, he wrote much poetry, many articles and plays himself, was President of many Highland Societies and championed the Gaelic language at every opportunity.*

Mum and Dad in courting days

The following belongs in my scrapbook, and must be attributed to an unknown bard, but it gives a sense of the person Mum married six years later, and is, I think, a picture of the time. Although she knew him as a young teenager on holiday in Skye, as their families were from the same small village, there were ten years of age between them, and they did not "court" until much later, and marry until he was 34 and she 24.)

IRRISOR-ES PEREANT

Mr Grant, our Gaelic and Latin teacher, is leaving us this Christmas for
Glasgow. The old order changeth; and thus the goodly fellowship of Mods
and Ceilidhs, School Sales and Christmas parties is dissolved – not to mention
certain fearful conclaves held in one classroom long after 4.20, screened from
the common gaze by Class 2's masterpiece – the new Waste Paper Box.
Mr Grant has done many things for us for whereof we are grateful. Though
his first Dochas faded in a purple vapour, we shall not forget him – or it! We
wish him success in his new work.

From his desk he rose at evening,
Bade farewell to haunts of labour,
Mystic sounds of Gaelic, Latin;
Bade farewell to all his pupils,
(Did not wake the ones that slumber'd):
Left them sadly conjugating,
Sauntered, whistling, through the doorway:
"I am going, O my pupils,
Off to Glasgow, off tomorrow!
Many blots and many howlers
Have I heard and seen among you.
Lest I come no more to l'arn you,
Don't forget to do your homework –
Page 1 – 60 – cave canem!"
And thus saying, he departed –
Through the leafy play-ground bounded;
O'er the H.G. gate he vaulted,
Union Street he left behind him,
Passed the gas works, starry, smelly,
Till the dust and wind together
Swept in eddies round about him;
Paused not till he crossed Argyll Street,
Reached his wigwam, Tigh-na-Mullan.
Out upon the golf course strode he,
Drove his Dunlop from the Club-house.
All the rabbits from the fairway

Leaped aside, and (at a distance)
Sat erect upon their haunches,
Saying to the Gaelic golfer:-
"Do not kill us, Gael, thou golfer!"
But he heeded not, nor heard them:
For his lost Dunlop he languished.
Searched each thicket, bunker, whin bush,
Till the evening sun descended,
And departing left behind it
One lone golfer, but no golf ball.
Homeward then he went without it,
Pondering sadly, and in this wise:-
"No more golf, as no more golf ball!"
Forth into the village went he,
Bade farewell to all his play mates,
Bade farewell to scenes of pleasure,
Scenes of pleasure and of triumph.
By the Institute he wandered,
Heard the billiards rippling near him;
Heard the racquets in the Drill Hall;
From the Wee School, strains of bagpipes.
Sighed, "Farewell, O my Lochgilphead!
No more Mods! – But one more ceilidh!"
Home once more went he for supper.
On the morrow, late uprising, Straight into Ardrishaig went he;
Scorning Links, MacBrayne's despising, With one stride a mile he measured.
On the pier he stood his suit case,
Turned and waved his hat at parting;
Hailed the Fusilier approaching O'er the dark and stormy waters.
Whispered to it, "Glasgow! Glasgow!" And (with luck) it darted forward.
"Beannachd leibh!" then screamed the sea gulls,
"Fare thee well! Good luck go with thee."
Thus departs our Gaelic teacher,
Latin teacher (Drill and Drawing), From his labours in Lochgilphead,
To the mighty city, Glasgow; Nearer to that Blessed Island,
Isle of Mists, and Isle of Mystery, Skye (the Highlander's Hereafter).

11. McGonigall (with apologies to Margaret and McGonigall)

There were four of us,
Flora, Betsy, Mary and me.
We each lived alone most of the time
And enjoyed each other's company.

To Duisdale church on a Sunday,
Sometimes only six of us there.
When that was sold (for a song),
To the parish church, Kilmore.
Mr MacDougall, faithful and true,
Lady MacDonald in the far-off pew.

Our little Morris to the WRI bound
Was often tightly packed.
Bella would join us as Iain nursed his knees –
There was always room for another to squeeze.

The shopping in Broadford was our outing,
Some lunch and a walkabout.
One called here, another there,
And afternoon tea in Mary's, Breakish,
Of that there was no doubt.

It was a good life,
Shared and enjoyed by all. ,
We weren't a clique, we called here and there,
Our friends varied and many, in whom all had a share.

I'm the last of our group,
I'm here and marking time.
I'm sure there are cups of tea in heaven
And wee drams to pass the time.

12. CEARCALL A' GHAOIL

A bit of self-indulgence in including a little bit of mediocre poetry which I wrote for a class at the Sabhal Mor Ostaig in Sleat – how pleased my Father would have been at the surge of interest in Gaelic in Sleat, and far beyond the College, the brain-child largely of Sir Iain Noble, which opened so near to Dad's birth-place three years after his death! I include the poem, as it represents the warm connection between no. 40 Camuscross and Struan Cottage across the Sound of Sleat in Airor.

Madainn chiuin Cheitein's mi ag eirigh gle thrath
A fine Spring morning and I awoke very early
Is leanaidh mi 'n rathad beag suas chun a' bhaigh,
  And I followed the little road up to the bay,
A cluintinn cail ach na h-eoin seinn cho binn
Hearing only the birds singing so sweetly
An aileadh cho urail – is mise leam fhin.
The atmosphere so fresh – and I by myself.

Shreap mi nas airde air an t-seann rathad beag
I climbed higher on the little old road
Air culaobh na taighean, faisg air monadh is creag.
Behind the houses, beside moor and rock.
Seallaidhean allain bho 'n mhullach a' bhaile
Beautiful vistas from the top of the village
Null thairis a chaoil sios gu Mallaig is Morar.
Over across the Sound down to Mallaig and Morar.

Rainig mi 'n taigh aig deireadh a' bhaile,
I reached the house at the end of the village,
Aireamh da-fhichead is dachaidh mo sheanmhair.
Number forty, and the home of my Grandmother.
Ach chunnaic mi fad as 'n taobh eile a' chaoil
But I saw far off on the other side of the Sound
Taigh ann an Cnodart a bha dachaidh mo sheanair.
A house in Knoydart which was the home of my Grandfather.

Dh'fhuirich mi 'n sud ann an aite as fhearr leam
I stayed there in the place most dear to me
A faireachdainn eachdraidh nan daoine is caomh leam.
Feeling the history of the people I love.
Na da linn ceangailte bho 'n da thaobh a' chaoil,
The two strands joined from the two sides of the Sound,
Is mise nam aonar ann an cearcall a' ghaoil.
And I solitary in a circle of love.

Looking to Knoydart from Kilmore Cemetery, Sleat

Part 3 Airor, Knoydart

Fact-finding & Recollections by Margaret Grant (daughter of Donald MacInnes of Airor, Knoydart)

1. Extracts from Deer Forest Commission

Angus MacInnes, son of Jonathan, or Eoin (Gaelic), went from Duisdalemore in Skye to Airor, Knoydart in 1835 to land previously occupied by Angus MacDonald who emigrated to America before the Clearances (1853 the time of the Clearances and the 3 families of MacInnes's must have been allowed to stay). The owner when these families went over to Airor was Mrs. MacDonnell of Glengarry. There are records of the terrible treatment meted out to her tenants at the time of the Clearances. It is strange that the people of Airor, including the MacInnes's, appear to have survived in the same area.

Certainly they had very small crofts, the houses close to the shore in most cases, rocky ground altogether.

In the Napier Report, the fifteenth sitting at Inverie, Knoydart on July 5th. 1894, witness Gillies MacKissock had been an applicant for land, and was refused first by Baird 3 years before, and now by Bowlby. Present at the sitting were George Gordon Esq., acting as chairman, Rev. Malcolm MacCallum, Henry Munro Esq. and William MacKenzie Esq., acting as secretary. Questioning him at this point was the lawyer for Bowlby, William MacKay.

MacKay	You tell us there was once a large population here and that they were evicted.
Gillies	Yes
MacKay	Did any of them remain here after they were evicted?
Gillies	Yes. They stopped on the estate in spite of them. I am a member of the family that stayed on the estate, in spite of the proprietor and proprietrix.
MacKay	How was that done?
Gillies	They managed it for 3 months sleeping under the shelter of walls and gardens, one place or another because if they put up a house, no matter how small or what shape, it would be broken down in 3 or 4 days' time. That way they lived from July to November. Then they got a sort of relief in the shape of tents which they used for 3 years.
MacKay	Who provided the tents?
Gillies	The people of Glasgow and Edinburgh, I fancy, sent them home and then again they would not be allowed to put them up in any place on the estate, but only on a small bit of ground that was attached to the Catholic Chapel at Sandaig.

MacKay	Did some put up a sort of shelter below high water mark?
Gillies	Yes. They always kept near the places where they had had crofts and houses, taking shelter about the walls of the house.
MacKay	So the evictions were attended by a great deal of cruelty?
Gillies	Yes. It was so hard that they could not get up a spark of fire to cook and had nothing to eat that day.
MacKay	Why was it that they were removed?
Gillies	For the rich farmer who wanted to get the land. Then it was to make way for the sheep.
MacKay	Who was the proprietor then?
Gillies	Mrs. MacDonald of Glengarry. They sold the estate soon after. The estate was sold in 1857 to Baird.
MacKay	You remember?
Gillies	I can't remember the date. To Mr James Baird, and the Bairds held it until last year, when Mr Bowlby bought it.

(In 1857 the estate was sold to Baird of Gartsherry, the ironmaster in Lanarkshire. At his death, he left property valued at £3,000,000. In 1871 he founded the Baird lectures for the defence of orthodox theology in Scotland and gifted £500,000 to the Church of Scotland. In 1893 the Knoydart Estate was sold to Bowlby.)

My (Margaret's) grand uncle, William MacInnes, aged 64, was then questioned. He was examined in Gaelic, through an interpreter.

MacKay	How many crofts in Airor?
William	There were 5 each end, but the number is now 8.
MacKay	What size?

William	Some 2 acres, others 1 and a half acres.
MacKay	Do you have sheep?
William	10 sheep.
MacKay	What is your rent?
William	£4.14/-
MacKay	What livestock do you have?
William	I'm entitled to 4 cows.
MacKay	Is there common hill ground?
William	Yes.
MacKay	Do you live mainly by your crofts?
William	No.
MacKay	What is your main occupation?
William	So long as Mr. Baird was here I carried the mails from Knoydart to Isleornsay. That is now discontinued. The letters go via Mallaig.
MacKay	Do the rest of the people here live on their crofts or are they fishermen?
William	They fish and go anywhere for labour. They are yachtsmen and sailors.
MacKay	Your crofts are too small to maintain a man and his family without other work?
William	The crofts are so small they wouldn't maintain one man for a year.
MacKay	Does your township want larger holdings?

William	Yes.
MacKay	Is there land there?
William	Yes. There was an extension of ground wanted at Samadalan for which we applied.
MacKay	Do you remember that Mr. Baird gave you herring nets?
William	He never gave me a net.
MacKay	Well, to some crofters?
William	I believe he did.
MacKay	The crofters in Airor are very well off, are they not?
William	Yes.
MacKay	But how?
William	They go far and near and even abroad to earn money for the families they leave at home. It is not the crofts at Airor that maintain the family.

A ruin on the road to Airor

MacKay	Do you not think it is better for them to do so than remain here on even larger crofts?
William	I think they could not stop at home, even if they had larger crofts. It would not do.
MacKay	Some of them have slated houses?
William	Yes, but if so, it was not by means of the produce of the crofts.
MacCallum	What sort of holding would you like for yourself? Would you be willing to move from the small croft you have and take a small farm if one was available in Knoydart?
William	Yes, if I could live on it.
MacCallum	Do you think that some such farms could be formed here?
William	Yes.
MacCallum	With regard to the slated houses in Airor, have they been built since the passing of the Crofters' Act?
William	Yes.
MacCallum	How many new houses?
William	Two.
MacCallum	And have these houses been put up by the earnings of the crofters' families south?
William	Yes.
Gordon	If you had got the extension to your croft you had applied for, would you have been content?
William	Yes. We thought we were to get it as Mr. Bowlby promised us, but now we have not got it, there is nothing for it but to look for another place.

MacKay	Do you know how many acres of pasture you crofters have between you?
William	I don't know.
MacKay	Would you agree with me that there are 1,000 acres?
William	I don't know anything about it.
MacKay	Until 1887 your rent was £6.5/-?
William	Yes.
MacKay	How long were you and those before you paying that rent?
William	Since 59 years.
MacKay	In 1887 it was reduced to £4.14/-?
William	Yes.
MacKay	And it is still your rent?
William	Yes.
MacKay	Your people were not originally from Knoydart?
William	No.
MacKay	Your father came, I think, from Skye?
William	Yes.
MacKay	And all the crofters in Airor, except one, came from Skye at the same time?
William	Yes. The parents of the present crofters.
MacKay	And they all settled there about the time of the evictions?
William	They came there before the tenants were removed from Knoydart?

MacKay	They were strangers at the time of the evictions?
William	Yes.
MacKay	And they were not removed?
William	No.
MacKay	Your father got land which before was in the possession of natives of Knoydart?
William	Yes.
MacCallum	But do you know whether the old natives were removed to make way for the colony from Sleat?
William	No.
Gordon	I would like to make this point quite clear. According to previous witnesses the evictions took place 41 years ago: according to you your father came from Skye 59 years ago: in other words, the people from Skye were in Knoydart 18 years previous to the evictions? One or two families left before the general clearances: these left of their own accord.
William	It was the land occupied by one who voluntarily left the place that my father got, but other colonists from Skye were in Airor before the general clearances. It was one Angus MacDonald who emigrated to America who had the land my father got.

Neil MacInnes, 71, my (Margaret's) grandfather was then questioned in Gaelic with an interpreter.

Gravestone of Neil and his wife Catherine at Kilmore, Sleat

The Knoydart MacInnes's are buried back on Skye

Gordon   Are you a crofter?

Neil   I have a croft in Airor.

Gordon   Did you hear the last witness's evidence?

Neil   Yes.

Gordon   And do you agree with the statement?

Neil   Yes.

Gordon   Have you anything further to add?

Neil   No, but I wish we could get what we applied for. I built a slated house at my own expense, myself and my sons, and my croft is the smallest in the township. It is my sons who are maintaining me and I am not owing one penny to the landlord or factor, neither did my father before me.

Gordon   Is there a general desire for larger holdings?

Neil	If we got what be applied for, we would be happy.
Gordon	You would have been content if you had got the addition you applied for at a fair rent?
Neil	Yes.

Jonathan MacInnes, 31, my (Margaret's) uncle, was then questioned in Gaelic with an interpreter.

Gordon	Are you a crofter in Airor?
Jonathan	Yes.
Gordon	Do you agree with the evidence from William MacInnes?
Jonathan	Yes.
Gordon	Do you have anything to add?
Jonathan	No.
MacCallum	What occupation do you follow?
Jonathan	I cannot follow any occupation. I must stay at home working the little croft.
MacCallum	Are you a fisherman?
Jonathan	Yes, I fish.
MacCallum	Do crofters and sons get employment in the forest?

Jonathan	No.
Munro	Where does the shooting tenant get his ghillies from if crofting sons are not so employed?
Jonathan	Any place he chooses to get them from. I don't think he would give the chance of employment to any from the district if they could avoid it.
MacKay	Were you not a ghillie yourself for a time?
Jonathan	I was for one year.
MacKay	When?
Jonathan	Two years ago.
MacKay	There was no shooting (for you) last year?
Jonathan	No.
MacKay	You don't know, but you may get employment this year?
Jonathan	I am quite sure I will not, if they can get it elsewhere.
MacKay	Who told you that?
Jonathan	No-one told me, but it is my opinion of the people who are in management.
MacKay	Is it not the same man as two years ago? The local factor is the same, is he not?
Jonathan	If so, he would not give me a chance.
MacKay	Don't you know any other Airor people who got employment?
Jonathan	No. They might for a month on a day's pay, that's all.
MacKay	Do you know Angus MacInnes?

Jonathan	Yes. He is there generally. He was out with me one day and told me he was in the service.
Mackay	Is he not from Airor?
Jonathan	Yes.
MacKay	Is he your brother?
Jonathan	No, a cousin.
MacKay	Then why did you say there was not one?
Jonathan	I did not think of him at the time, but I am quite sure there is no other form Airor.
MacKay	Perhaps if you thought a little longer you could remember more?
Jonathan	I am quite sure I would not. They would be very sorry to give us the chance of employment.
MacKay	Do you know a man, Donald MacDonald, who was a shepherd at Scotas?
Jonathan	Yes.
MacKay	Is he a native of Airor?
Jonathan	It is from Airor he was.
MacKay	So there was no difference made so far as the people of Airor are concerned between them and the other townships?
Jonathan	Yes, there was. Ever since we applied to the Crofters' Commission they have turned against us as much as they could.
MacKay	Do you know that Mr Bowlby was not aware until I was here three weeks ago that you had gone to the Crofters' Commission? Or even Mr Cumming?

Jonathan	I am quite satisfied that Mr Bowlby would do rightly, but the man who is acting under him would not allow him to do so.

2. Recollections

Going back to her grandfather, Neil's, questioning in the Deer Forest Commission, Margaret continues:-

You can imagine that I was proud to read in print, in the report, these words of my Grandfather, Neil MacInnes. He and his brother, Calum, built new homes, I suppose when they married, Calum at Braevalla and Neil, Struan, the old home midway or so, and in ruins. Calum's house was left by the family around 1930 and became in ruins, but Struan, well built and maintained, with a porch added at the front, was sold to the estate in the 1960's by some of the MacInnes family for around £200, and sold again by the estate around 1984 for £14,000.

Struan Cottage, 1894

There was a beautiful garden there in my young days, the 1920's and 1930's, roses, peony roses, shrubs, a variety of flowers and even arum lilies. Joan, the youngest of Neil's family, made this her joy – a relaxation after the labour of potato-planting and hay-making. The garden was hedged, with gates either side and at the front leading on to the cart road. Below the road, and on a slope, there was a further enclosure with black and red currant bushes, rhubarb and some vegetables. There was an apple tree there and one in the garden. A burn ran beside the house, hence the name "Struan" (Gaelic for a stream). This was convenient for the erection of a "tigh beag" (toilet).

There were plant pots on the shelves on either side of the porch. On the right of the house was the sitting room or parlour, kept for special occasions, on the left, the kitchen, the living room, In one corner of it was the meal and flour chest, with the dresser with the plate rack, and in front of the window was the "trush" (truinns), a wooden seat similar to a garden seat. Off the kitchen there was a small room, the closet (closaid), which had been a tiny bedroom and was now the scullery, storing crockery, pots and utensils.

From the narrow hall, there was a beautiful, polished, wooden staircase – the work of John MacInnes, son of Neil. Untrained, but clever with a knife and wood, he made intricate picture frames, shepherds' crooks, and I recollect a walking stick with a serpent twisted round beyond the dividing wall.

At the back of the house was a room built on: a stone floor and stone shelf with milk basins set out. The cream was removed with a scallop shell, put into a tall earthen jar, collected for several days till on the turn, then churned. There was a tall wooden churn with a long-handled plunger. Just before the butter would appear, some cream would be removed and this served with oatmeal – stapag – lovely with brambles!

Neil MacInnes and his wife, Catriona, who was a MacKinnon from Camuscross, Skye, daughter of the Cooper had fourteen of a family. Catriona died in 1891, aged 51, and Neil died in 1903 aged 80. The first death in that family was in 1932 when John died aged 70 years. This was quite remarkable considering the times in which they grew up.

John was the oldest of the family, my father, Donald, the next. Their diet must have been good, milk, butter, cheese, scones, eggs and fish – plenty fish: beautiful fresh fish straight from the sea. I haven't tasted any to equal it! My father's cousin, Jimmy, on a visit to Airor from Camuscross, is pictured bringing the fish from the sea, my Aunt Kate cleaning them, putting the fish in one pail. The roe and liver she put in a basin and with that she mixed onions and oatmeal, made fish soup, dropped balls of the mixture in, and what wasn't used then could be fried. Not only did my Aunt make strong-smelling, strong-tasted cheese, but later she added to it caraway seed sent by her sisters in the south! Many liked it, but I couldn't!

Their washing was done in the burn and blanket washing was a day for work and picnic: also the peat-cutting. Aunt Kate assumed, or perhaps was forced to assume the mother's duties. She looked after the youngest members, supported financially by her brothers who were working south, with lesser support from the sisters in the same position, as could be expected, rates for women being different; moral support was strong. The male members of the family were certainly tied with their obligation, and those who did marry were older when they did so; my father was approaching forty when he married. I think he would have had to face his sisters with courage!

The youngest son, Eoin, remained at home on the croft all his life, with occasional trips south, once walking or riding a horse to Ayrshire. Kate was in charge and Joan, the youngest, also spent her life there, until she came south after Eoin's death. Kate had died earlier and so the house went back to the estate, and for that my Aunt would get £200, if she was lucky.

Going back in time, Neil and Malcolm, sons of Angus, had a large fishing boat, which sometimes went as far as Ireland. Later Neil was a fisherman at Inverie with Bowlby. William, their brother, came to Isleornsay three times weekly with mail. He moved from the middle ruined house to Samaladan when he married. Malcolm, Braevalla, brought a pair of horses, a plough and a harrow over in a boat to do a week's work in Camuscross. What sailors they must have been!

Eoin, son of Malcolm, married his brother's fiancée at the dying request of his brother. They had three in the family and Eoin's sister, Janet, lived with them. As a girl on holiday with my Aunts, I loved going there.

The sad thing is that out of a family of fourteen, there is only one great grandson – and he is in America, the son of Judge Donald MacInnes. However, I'm sure the good genes have been passed on through the female line and let's hope some force for good.

A gathering of cousins at the now-occupied Struan, April 2013

Two stories told to me by Isobel MacInnes, told to her by her father, John, son of Angus.

In a cove beyond the bridge, on the other side of the Struan byre, there appeared to some people, at individual times, a fellow with brass buttons – "fear a phuitean bhuidhe".

Isobel's father, was walking across the hill, the Mam, from Airor to Inverie. His companion told him to stand aside, as a funeral was passing. Her father couldn't see it. His companion said, "Put your foot on mine and you will see it too". But he didn't do so.

Recollections of Cathie Jack (nee MacInnes) – written down by her sister, Margaret.

From Cardross, Cathie, Iain and their Mother and Father would be collected by Fraser in his horse and cab. They took with them four or six loaves for Airor, and Mother always made gooseberry jelly before leaving. The train to Mallaig and one time she remembered going directly across to Camuscross from Mallaig, when the boat with passengers had to heave to in a storm. It was about 1.30am when they arrived at no 40.

The small ferry boat came out at Isleornsay with the two ferrymen with lanterns.

They left Skye early on the mail boat to Inverie, and there Uncle Eoin would meet them with the horse and trap. One time a storm arose going in the small open mailboat from Mallaig. The woman sitting beside Mother said, " Oh my God!" each time the boat hit the waves and Cathie was crying, held between her Father's knees, as he co-operated with the sailor. Mother was silent and fearful. She hated small boats – her uncle, and her only brother at the age of twenty-one, had been drowned at sea.

3. Odd Newscuttings about Knoydart (unfortunately no dates given, although some can be worked out)

On Friday last there were laid to rest in Kilmore, Skye, the remains of the late Mr Wm. MacInnes, (Uncle of the "14") Samaladan, Knoydart, who died at the advanced age of 79. Before the Mallaig Railway was opened, Mr MacInnes carried for a long number of years the Knoydart mails between Isle Ornsay and Airor.

To mark the coming-of-age of his elder son and heir, the Hon. Ronald Nall-Cain, Lord Brocket yesterday entertained 150 guests on his 50,000-acre Knoydart estate, West Inverness-shire.

The gathering – which included tenants, employees and neighbours from Mallaig – heard from their host about the prospect of further improvements being carried out on the estate in the New Year under the Hill Farming Act.

Lord Brocket also announced that an estate club was being formed.

Then, on behalf of the tenants, Mr. Jonathan MacInnes, (cousin of the "14", son of Malcolm) who has lived on the estate for 63 years, presented the Hon. Ronald with salmon-fishing tackle and a cheque for £25.

Thirty-five school children had fun and games at an afternoon party, at which each child received an electric torch after a deer-stalker's crook had been presented to "Mr Ronald".

And the grown-ups wound up the day's festivities by dancing at a ball at Knoydart House.

ARNISDALE – Mr Angus MacInnes, (no. 3 of "14") head gamekeeper to the late Major V. Fleming Of Arnisdale Deer Forest, has been appointed head gamekeeper to Sir A. Nicolson of Arisaig. He leaves this district with the best wishes of the community; and during his stay of four years he was highly esteemed.

DESTRUCTIVE LANDSLIP AT GLENQUOICH – ONE MAN KILLED

A thunderstorm of a severe and unprecedented character took place in this district on the afternoon of Sunday, accompanied by floods of an equally exceptional and violent nature. The Kingie Forest, rented by Lord Burton, along with Glenquoich, suffered severely from landslips, the amount of which seems almost incredible on Scur-an-uaran, Corrybuie and Kingie hill sides.

The house of Mr. John Henderson, his Lordship's stalker at Corrybuie, situated on the right bank of the Corry burn, which runs into Loch Quoich some two hundred yards below, was, together with the adjoining grounds and outbuildings, assailed by an enormous tornado of mud, water, etc., carrying in its course huge boulders of stone several tons in weight.

It being Sunday, the sole occupants of the place were two roadmen, who stayed at home in the workmen's bothy that day. As this erection, along with the barn and cow-byre, was suddenly demolished, one of the men, Mr A. MacInnes, *(Alexander, cousin of "14", son of Malcolm)* was swept away along with it and killed. The deceased was a native of Knoydart, a man of amiable disposition, and much respected. The sad news of his melancholy death has cast quite a gloom over the glen. All efforts to recover the body up to the present have been unsuccessful.

Mr John Henderson, stalker, has sustained heavy losses, all his furniture, utensils and general household furniture being carried away, along with several calves, and a brace of valuable sporting dogs. His croft and potato field are entirely covered with gravel, slag, and large stones, averaging in depth from two to eight feet. Much sympathy is felt for himself and Mrs Henderson under the sad circumstances. Their losses may be computed at a figure somewhat over £60.

KNOYDART – PRESENTATION

On Friday of last week Mr MacDonald, missionary, was met at Airor by a few friends and presented with a purse of sovereigns, contributed by the congregation, on the occasion of his leaving the district owing to the vacancy being now filled. Mr Bowlby of Knoydart contributed handsomely to the presentation fund. Mr MacDonald has also been the recipient of a handsomely carved walking stick, the workmanship of Mr John MacInnes, Struan Cottage, Airor, *(probably no. 1 of the "14")*.

ARISAIG – MARRIAGE

On the forenoon of Wednesday last week, there was celebrated in Arisaig Hotel the marriage of Mr Angus MacInnes *(no. 3 of "14"),* Drumindarroch, and Miss Annie Grant, Broadford, Isle of Skye, both well-known and highly regarded in the district. The ceremony was performed by the Rev. H. MacKenzie Campbell. Miss Campbell, Arisaig Hotel, acted as bridesmaid; while the duties of groomsman fell to Mr Wm. Grant, Borrowdale. The bride looked exceedingly well in a dress of white voile, with orange blossom. After the marriage cake and wine were handed round, and the toast of the newly-married was heartily honoured. The whole company then retired to the dining-room, where an elaborate luncheon was served. The table decorations were in excellent taste, and no pains had been spared to make everything a success. Various toasts were proposed; and amongst others "The Host and Hostess, Mr and Mrs Maclure," by Mr Wm. Grant, Borrowdale. The young couple left for the south by the afternoon train, receiving an enthusiastic send-off, both at the hotel and afterwards at the railway station. Bagpipe music was supplied by Messrs Fraser and Robertson. At the special request of the bride and bridegroom, the party remained for a few hours longer to celebrate the event in music and dancing

Driving to Church in Airor, Knoydart

KNOYDART The winter Sacrament was held in the Church of Scotland at Inverie on Sunday, September 25. The weather was favourable and by the kindness of the factor, Mr MacLeod, several were taken by "Land Rover" from Airor, 14 dangerous miles of rocky road. The services were attended by the shooting tenants from Glaschoille, Sir John and Lady Stainton and family, and by the shooting tenants at Inverie Lodge, Mr and Mrs Baird and family and guests. Miss Luvina Baird played the organ at both services. One communicant joined the Church by profession of faith for the first time. The officiating minister was Rev. Robert P. Aitchison, Mallaig, and he was assisted by the elders, Messrs Jonathan MacInnes *(Braeval ?)* and John MacDonald.

AIROR IS A DIFFERENT PLACE JUST NOW

Vivid memories of Airor, Knoydart have been recalled to another native of that remote locality by the article recently contributed to the "People's Journal" by Angus MacInnes. *(? had to be born around 1884)*

Mrs Downie, 60 King Street, Crieff (formerly Jessie MacInnes, *(no. 12 of "14")* of Struan Cottage, Airor), says the writer of the article himself, though he may not recall it, shared a school bench with her in Airor School.

"Many a time he played the Good Samaritan when I was having difficulty with my spelling and my arithmetic. I well remember, too, his sister, who was schoolmistress there, and I have in my possession a photograph of her at this particular time.

"William MacInnes was my uncle, and owned the horse named Davie. As the writer has mentioned, he was a very able seaman, and he needed to be for one of his main jobs was the bringing of the mail from Isle Ornsay across the Sound of Sleat to Airor.

"Many a rough crossing he had, many an anxious vigil was kept by those who awaited his return, for only a storm of exceptional severity prevented his setting out.

"Diamond belonged to my cousin, Jonathan MacInnes, of Braeval. In these days horses were very important members of such a community, for the major part of the work of a croft was done by the horse. It was also our dependable means of transport, for the nearest church was seven miles away at Inverie.

"The passing of the years has wrought great changes in Airor. It is now an almost deserted community, but perhaps in the not too distant future the silent and disused schoolroom will once again echo to children's voices and laughter as it did in the happy days of long ago."

4. **By Airor stream.** *This poem is in memory of an un-named relative.*

By Airor stream that gently flows
She first did see the light
Mid flowers that grew on Airor banks
To roam was her delight.

Fair as the lily in the shade
She day by day grew up
And year by year the gentle maid
Had joys to fill her cup.

By Airor streams that sweetly sing
She saw another light
That to the heart does gladness bring
And fills with holy light.

On Horeb's top she gladly stood
And viewed the pleasant land,
And with her Saviour crossed the flood
To join the Immortal band.

By Airor stream that gently slows
Our lily had its rise
But now in other climes it grows
More fair in Paradise.

PART 4. TO THE UNITED STATES

1. Carolyn's Recollections and poetry

As with so many families from the Gaidhealtachd, ours was no different in the scattering of people world-wide.

One of the sisters, Christina, married in Skye and in 1904 set sail from there for America and a new life. We have the good fortune to have many warm connections with our trans-Atlantic cousins, and Carolyn wrote the following vivid and touching account of her Grandmother's settling in New York State.

When my grandmother Christina MacKinnon arrived in America with two young children Margaret and Mary and baby Neilina it was a far cry from the beauty of Skye. She often told me that when leaving Skye the villagers came out waving sheets and singing "Will Ye No Come Back Again?" She also told me of the kindness of the ship's porter who would bring milk to her for the baby who was sick. She had already buried one child Donald in Scotland and Neilina would also later die. Upon arriving at Ellis Island they had to stay overnight before making their way to Ogden Street in Newark. When she would show me pictures of Scotland she would say to me "can you imagine leaving that for a place where I would look out the window to other peoples' laundry and different languages spoken all around you."

My grandfather Neil McKinnon whose sister had come over and encouraged him to come, had gotten a job with Coats, later Coats and Clark and after a life at sea on Vanderbilt's yacht where he was away from his family having gone around the world twice, this was a chance to settle down. My grandmother and grandfather bought a house in Kearny on Highland Avenue, a big Victorian house, equipped with gas lamps that had room for chickens out back.

My grandparents had three more girls; Catherine, my mother. Elizabeth, who just passed away in June at the age of 101, and Ina who is 98.

They joined a United Presbyterian Church in Newark, NJ, a stricter Presbyterian church where only Psalms were sung rather than hymns. It was thought of as a Scottish Presbyterian church and just as Kearny had a lot of Scots so did this church. This would change later but I remember my grandmother keeping a strict Sabbath and when my mother and aunts were children it was even stricter. They were to only read two books, one a religious book and one a

80

nature book or the Bible on Sunday. My Grandmother told me that, growing up, her own mother was very strict and she was very dour. We were told the story of Mary Kennedy her mother walking miles to receive communion. She was a member of the Wee Free church. My grandmother loosened a bit later. She allowed her grandchildren to listen to the dramatized stories in the Bible that were broadcast over the radio on Sunday evenings. Decades later my brother was able to persuade her that God wouldn't mind if she watched a western show Bonanza on Sunday nights. A funny story here though. When my grandmother was visiting my Ina at their shore place she accepted a wee dram of sherry, a rare thing for her. Just as she took a sip Ina noticed her minister coming up the walk. At which point my grandmother hid her glass under the chair. Her Wee Free upbringing kicked in.

My grandmother kept ties to Scotland through attending the Daughters of Scotia and the Skye Society early on. I think though that her major activities centered around her church and her family. Having grown up by the sea my grandparents loved the ocean and built a small house down at the Jersey shore for vacations. It looks in the pictures I have seen to be the size of a small croft cottage. It was just the outside shell they purchased and Poppy had to build the inside. My mother remembers Poppy my grandfather would bring lumber down on the train to add to the cottage. When the children were still at home my Grandmother bought a new house just being built on Bel-grove drive in Kearny. My mother remembered her mother taking her for a walk and showing her the house and that there was then a view all the way to the river. It was a two family house and that is where my mother, father and brother and I lived on the first floor with my Grandmother and Aunt Margaret upstairs.

The sisters as they became old enough to work all contributed to the household. My mother would tell me of her excitement upon seeing Margaret get off the bus from work carrying material because she then knew she would be getting a new dress. Mary, Elizabeth and my mother only went through two years of high school so that they could get jobs. Ina was the only sister to complete 4 years of high school. Ina was also the sister that was able to get her mother to attend a school program. Apparently she was shy about going and Ina tells me she said that all the other mothers go and it would mean so much to her if her mother would be there. She said she did come, complete with gloves and hat and Ina told her mother how proud she was that she was there. Apparently my grandparents would speak Gaelic to each other. My aunt Betty remembers asking my grandmother not to speak Gaelic when she was having a friend over. She remembers saying "my friend might think you're Italian!" Obviously a prejudice of the times.

I loved growing up with my grandmother upstairs. It was a constant source of nurture and security for me and also a source of entertainment. However when DuPont moved to Wilmington my grandmother moved into an apartment for a short time with Margaret. She was not happy there and I was very sad that she was away and was ecstatic when she moved back. I know she had some wonderful visits with the MacInnes's in Kennett Square, PA, which was near Wilmington during that time. Later I remember Joan and Naida coming to visit. Grandma was also very fond of Dr Purdy the minister of the church they attended. When I was still quite young I would love to watch my grandmother cook. I would love to watch her cut up vegetables for soup or make one of her one pot meals. When I would ask her what was cooking she would say what sounded like tortoise and fat in the kale pat. Translation taters and fat in the kale pot. My grandmother would give me a small "taste" on a plate of whatever she was cooking. I much preferred her cooking to my mother's but possibly it was because by the time our dinner time came I had already eaten with Grandma.

My grandmother had visitors that would come to see her. There were the two Jimmy's. One a tall Jim and the other a short Jim. There was Mrs. Stewart or Mrs. MacManus. Or Roy Stevenson when his ship was in on the Cunard Line. All Scots. There were times when my grandmother's knees were bad and I would run upstairs and then run down her staircase so that her visitors would be let into her front door. Or I would go upstairs to run down and get her mail. Oh and the excitement when those thin almost onion skinned blue envelopes would arrive from the "other side", I knew how happy this would make my grandmother because it would be from Rachel, Lizzie or from Maggie with news. I knew that her only visit back to Skye had been with Elizabeth and Ina when they stayed in No 40.

Of course living in Grandmas house meant I would get to see all my Aunt and cousins as well when they came to visit. I learned to put the kettle on very soon after someone's arrival. I learned to make tea properly by hotting the pot first. I learned hospitality required offering something to eat even if the visitor only had time for a spot of tea.

Aunt Maggie's visit was wonderful for my grandmother and for all of us. The McCarthy hearings were going on at the time and they were glued to the TV watching and discussing it. Although I can't remember the content of their conversations I loved any excuse to be around them as they visited with each other. I remember feeling close to Maggie. Both she and my grandmother had a quiet presence that to a child was comforting.

Aunt Christina and Margaret's mother in the backyard in Newark, New Jersey

I grew up with a grandmother who I knew to be very interested in current events both in the newspapers and TV. We were able to watch Elizabeth's coronation. Poppy was active in local politics and was a Republican. Grandma told me she deemed herself a Rockefeller Republican which to me meant she was more liberal. Although it took some arm twisting by my Aunt to get my Grandmother to accept Medicare once it went into effect. She also enjoyed reading westerns just as she enjoyed watching them on TV. If I was going to the library she would ask me to pick up a western or two.

What was most evident to me in my grandmother was her strong faith. It wasn't an easy faith but one that she worked on. If I would run upstairs to say goodnight I might come upon her, her long hair taken down from her bun, brushed and braided, lying in bed and reading the Bible. She often read from the Psalms. An important verse for her was "trust in The Lord with all thine heart and lean not unto thine own understanding, in all thy ways acknowledge Him and he shall direct thy path." I think she held onto that verse as it took a certain courage to leave her home and family and follow her husband to America creating her own family of 5 daughters, 12 grandchildren, 27 great grandchildren and many great-great grandchildren.

The following are two poems written by Carolyn.
<u>GAELIC</u>

You never forgot the language
I would hear you
humming it under your breath
as I came upon you quietly,
catching briefly
the rhythm and cadence
of some mournful tune
some lighter reel.
But the language
you hid from me
except when Katie came
and spoke the Gaelic
naturally and unabashed.
Then I would ask you
to teach me some words
a few phrases.
Did you bury the language
to quiet your grief?
Or did you hold it
precious and private
and close to you
to croon for your particular comfort
as you remembered
the heather and the hills,

the lochs and the sea,
the bens and the burns
sung about
in that strange and foreign tongue
you left behind
when you came to America

Skye

Aird, Ord, Breakish
Staffin, The Quirang
Ardvasar, Armadale, Sleat
The words resound in my mind
as the everlasting sea resounds
against the shores of this
haunting timeless isle
Resounding then whispering
while the sea ebbs and flows
Calling, Calling
bidding our return
as the gorse blooms yellow
on moors and near woods
yielding up primroses and bluebells
Promising the brown hills
will soften o heather

Soon, Soon
and we should walk,
walk in the steps of ancestors
whose surefooted strength echoes
from the Braes to Ben-Na-Callich
from the crofts to the Cuillins
Come Home.

2. Joanne Petrie

Mum was always interested in the wide spread of the family and the rich diversity that can develop. The following is my own short summary of the influential career in the States of a cousin, whose Grandmother, on the other side of our family, also went to the States from Skye.

Joanne Petrie, married to a Russian scientist who had fled the Soviet Union, was a lawyer in the Department of Transportation in the US Government, eventually specialising in time zones and daylight saving time. She became known as "Mother Time" as she mediated in disputes between states.
In the 1880's, the continental US was divided by the railroads into four primary time zones, and this was made Federal Law in 1918. Daylight saving

time was used during the periods of the two World Wars, but after 1945 it was left up to each community to decide if they wanted to continue it or not, which led to considerable confusion across the country. It was 1967 before daylight saving time finally became standardised throughout most of the USA, and the Transportation Department was charged with being the nation's timekeeper. It was Joanne who upheld this. She also understood the personal nature to some people of time zones – when you got up or the time you went to school mattered. She mediated at many public meetings and listened to local disputes.

Joanne had a particular hobby which was in keeping with her character – she performed as a flamenco dancer internationally. She led a lively and varied life until her untimely death in 2013 at the age of 55.

A fascinating lady, only two generations from Camuscross on the Isle of Skye.

I AM BACK

Written about the age of 83, on one of her visits north to Camuscross, from her retirement home in Abbeyfield in Helensburgh.

I am back. Back home, that is. A chance of a lift and the kindly fellow brought me right here. And the sun shone as we arrived, though the rain had been very heavy most of the way. A quick cuppa for the Good Samaritan (minus milk, which I'd forgotten to bring), and he leaves. I gather my thoughts and air my bed and open the windows and mull over the charge on the Skye Bridge. It is excessive. One pound should be the fare for a small car and the rest of the annual repayment to the private firm should come from the government. Whichever government! A pleasant interruption: my kindly neighbour with a bag of kindling for my fire, and a return trip with milk. Not just over the wall! There is a channel of sea between us which means a round trip. Not far and no bother to my good Yorkshire neighbour. I like – very much appreciate – my "white settler" neighbours. A Yorkshire man is just as kindly as a Skye man, and this one and his wife are assets in our village.

I've had a good night's sleep – to bed late, up fairly early. Porridge from my own pan tastes good, as does my tea with milk. Light the coal fire, which with a little attention, paper held in front, burns brightly. No need for a large fire – the sun is shining. And as I wash my dishes (last night's as well), I see that seagull standing on the high point of the rock, the water grey blue as there is quite a bit of cloud and mist over the high hills, but the lighthouse stands out clearly.

That seagull has been appearing regularly over the years. Is it the same one? Of course there are others, but he is the only one who faces houseward and looks in my windows. I've been a widow now for twenty-six years. Still I've a good memory and good memories. The seagull has been coming for a long time. I wonder does he come when I'm south in my retirement home? I always see him when I come back.

One final remark!

This little lark is certainly a good excuse to leave housework, though it does interfere with Scrabble.